Conte

KU-327-670

****

Chapter 1 - Getting Started

Introduction

An autobiography is about sharing: sharing your experiences, sharing your thoughts, opinions, feelings and emotions and sharing lessons from the past. Your memories are important and certainly worth writing down, but they will only be of lasting value if you write them in such a way that you encourage other people to read them. This book has been written for anyone who feels they have a story to tell but who needs help remembering the details, writing in an engaging fashion or organising and structuring their material. Who knows: if you produce a well written body of work, it may even motivate other people to follow your example and write about their own lives as well.

Having decided to take the plunge and start putting your life down on paper, it can be quite a daunting prospect. If you were in your 20s and had a good memory, you would have 20 x 365 days worth of material to work with. So where does that leave anyone who is well over 50?

Fortunately, an autobiography can only be a snapshot of the most interesting, unusual or important parts of your life. This book will help you decide what to include and help you achieve your aims by looking at your reasons for writing, your likely audience and what you can do to make the whole process manageable and enjoyable.

Remembering

One reason people give for not writing their autobiography is that they feel their memory isn't good enough. Memories are so elusive; you may have already decided that most of the important details of your past life are lost forever in the mists of time. I am glad to tell you that there are techniques available to overcome this problem if it is your main concern. I will introduce you to a wide range of different approaches that will help jog your memory, and you should end up with more than enough material to work on.

Research

A later chapter looks at various methods for carrying out research, but it is worth noting here that it would be sad if you saw autobiography in terms of simply a description of events interspersed with facts and figures. Together with the facts themselves, it is your chance to convey your feelings, views, opinions and emotions as events unfolded, as well as how these have changed over time. Your readers will often be far more excited by the personality of the writer and how life has affected them than by any dates and times. On the other hand, inaccuracies and incorrect information can be annoying and misleading. So you will learn where you can go to check up on details if these will improve and inform your writing.

Activities

Throughout each chapter, you will be asked to carry out a number of activities. To get the most out of this book and ultimately achieve your goal, it is important that you complete them at the appropriate time. They are there to build on the ideas presented earlier and will help you clarify your thoughts as well as practise the skills required to produce good quality autobiographical writing.

Book structure

This book will:

- Help you identify your real reasons for writing an autobiography
- Introduce a wide variety of techniques that you can use in order to remember details from your past
- Help you start writing your memories down
- Demonstrate methods for improving your writing so that it comes to life
- Guide you through the various sources of further information
- Suggest different methods for structuring your finished work
- Point out the pitfalls when it comes to editing your material
- Identify ways to publish all or parts of your life story

Each chapter follows a similar pattern:

- An introduction to the main themes and ideas for tackling them in your own work
- Activities for you to carry out that will get you remembering and writing
- One piece of work to complete at the end of the chapter where you can apply the various skills or ideas that have been introduced.

Expectations

No assumptions are made in this book about what you want to achieve or what type of writer you are. You may prefer to work towards a full autobiography that will one day be published, or you may decide to use the ideas I introduce to help you fill in gaps or organise material you already have. You may like the idea of writing up a limited number of memories or your aim may simply be to get over writer's block or practise your writing skills using ready-made material. Whatever you want to do, this book will be able to help you.

Some examples of shorter pieces of writing based on your life story that may appeal to you include:

- Character sketches of people you knew
- Descriptions of past times
- Essays on your views about particular aspects of life
- Short stories based around real events
- Poems
- Articles for magazines and journals
- Step-by-step instructions
- Tips and tricks based on past experience

If you are determined to produce a book, short pieces such as those listed above that are organised in a coherent way could still end up being bound. Just think of all the diaries and journals that fill today's bookshelves.

Whatever material you produce, you need to prepare yourself for three things:

1. Honesty: Without hurting anyone's feelings unnecessarily, most people would agree that it is important for future generations that any non-fiction autobiographical writing is as accurate and truthful as you can make it.

2. Uncovering the bad as well as the good: When you delve into the past, feelings are likely to emerge that were deeply buried and that may be painful or disturbing.

3. Rewriting: The quicker you can put your memories down on paper the better, so when you first start you can ignore style, grammar or spelling and just write it all down. However, for other people to enjoy reading your work you are going to have to cut out some things or move them around, edit carefully and spend time producing finished work of a high enough standard.

Reasons for writing

Activity 1

Write down your main reason for writing about your life.

For a complex task like writing an autobiography, motivation is a key factor. There are a number of reasons why you might want to write your life story, all of which are positive ones that should carry you through to your ultimate goal.

These include:

• Wanting to communicate and/or be a writer

Aspiring novelists are always being told to "write about what you know", so autobiography must be one of the best ways to start out on a writing career.

- Therapy, or for personal development

There is nothing like exploring the past to clarify your thoughts, develop self-knowledge and throw up a fresh view of yourself. It can also lead to "closure" on a difficult episode in your life.

- To collate material you have already gathered

Perhaps you have a trunk full of letters, diaries, photos and other memorabilia that you would love to get into some sort of order.

- To record or illustrate a particular time or event

Some of the most enthralling accounts of our history have only come to us in the form of autobiographical writing. If you have lived through a time such as a war, a natural disaster, the depression or "the sixties", for example, your own experience will add to the general body of knowledge. Or you may want to describe a significant personal episode at first hand and share your thoughts about it.

- To be remembered

We all regret the passing of friends or relatives before we have had a chance to get to know them properly, and so perhaps we all owe the next generation at least a glimpse into our own lives.

- Because you have been inspired

With so much interest in genealogy and family history, including television programmes such as *Who Do You*

Think You Are? you may be excited at the prospect of researching into your own background.

- To connect to a younger generation

It is surprising how much it can mean to read the thoughts or childhood memories of a parent or grandparent, and how much closer it can bring you.

Other reasons

If you have listed other reasons, it is important to be realistic about them. For example you may have written down that:

- You have been asked to write your autobiography by others

If this is the case, it is important to 'own' the material or you could lose your motivation and perhaps never finish.

- You want to make money

Sadly, unless you are a celebrity or have some gruesome skeletons in the family cupboard, the ordinary life of an ordinary person may not be exciting enough for publishers or film studios. In that case, the only answer is to produce the most brilliantly written autobiography possible, so that people will still want to read it.

In one sense, it is quite possible to make money from autobiography and that is by creating saleable material of some sort that is *based* on your life. Examples include non-fiction articles and talks as well as short stories, poems or plays. Some of these ideas are looked at in more detail in a later chapter.

- Revenge

If this is your real reason, you should take great care. Not only are there laws of libel but this type of story usually does little for your own self-esteem and can reflect badly on you when others read it.

- To write the story of a fascinating relative

This is where autobiography may well cross over into biography and it will no longer be *your* story. As long as you are happy about this, then this book will be just as helpful to you in completing your task.

Where are you now?

Before working through the material, it may help to analyse what you have done so far to prepare yourself for the task ahead.

Activity 2

Note down exactly what steps you have taken, if any, towards writing your life story.

You may have done quite a bit, but for those of you facing a blank piece of paper, don't forget that there is more to building up a picture of your life than just writing down everything you can remember. Useful activities include:

- speaking recently to a relative or friend about your shared past, which may have triggered a few memories

- Gathering together various items such as photos, letters or other mementoes from the past that will help you think back to earlier times

- Jotting down some headings under which you would like to write a little about your life

- Revisiting a place you once lived or spent some time and comparing it to how it was then

- Seeing an exhibition or wandering through a museum that has reminded you of your childhood house, the clothes you wore, work activities or other aspects of the past.

Stumbling blocks

In case you have tried, and failed, to write an autobiography before, here are a few reasons people give for *not* doing so:

- Their English is not good enough
- They don't write well enough
- Their memory is too poor
- They are overwhelmed by too much material
- Their life is too boring
- They are not famous enough
- There is nowhere they can sit quietly and get on with it
- They don't have enough time
- They cannot use a computer

If any of these statements apply to you, read the next points carefully:

1. Chapter 9 will introduce you to various techniques to improve your grammar, punctuation and spelling.
2. Chapters 5 & 6 will give you lots of simple ideas to make your writing more interesting and enjoyable to read
3. Working through Chapters 3 & 4 should give you lots of help in jogging your memory.
4. The whole of Chapter 8 is devoted to helping you get your life story into a manageable order.
5. Are *your* grandparents or great-grandparents too boring to read about? I don't imagine you think so, as anything you can learn about them adds to your understanding of your own history. The same is therefore true of your descendants who will be equally fascinated by what you write down.
6. To your own family at least, you are as important as any celebrity, (but don't expect mainstream publishers to necessarily agree, if you are hoping to produce a best seller).

<u>Where and when to work</u>

Activity 3

For this activity, imagine yourself starting work on some autobiographical writing.

1. Where will you be working?
2. When will you be working?

Where to work

Telling ourselves that we are unable to find a quiet place to write is sadly a common technique that is deployed when we are afraid to do something difficult. If J.K.Rowling can sit in noisy cafes and end up writing seven Harry Potter books, most of us with a home or at least a room of our own should be able to manage better. You simply need the strength to insist that you set aside a *small space* where your pens and papers won't need to be continually cleared away (so the dining table is not as good as a small desk under the stairs), and that you are allowed at least an hour or so each week when you can be undisturbed. If there really is nowhere at home, public libraries are a good alternative.

The ideal is a room where you can sit and work quietly, and where you can keep all the materials you need around you. If that is not possible, aim for the most pleasant space you can find where you won't be disturbed.

If you have to move your work regularly (for example if you are working on the kitchen table), it will help to buy a large box file in which you can quickly stow away your books and papers ready for the next session.

Finding Time

For busy people, finding enough time for the task ahead can be daunting. However, it is amazing how much time we all waste that could be put to much better use in writing an autobiography.

*

Activity 4 – The Golden Square

Draw the following labeled squares (overleaf) out on a piece of paper and fill in your own examples (try to find at least 5 for **both** NOT URGENT squares):

	URGENT	**NOT URGENT**
IMPORTANT	*Dentist appointment* *Catching a train* *Attending a meeting* *Taking children to school*	*Keeping fit e.g. going swimming* *Meditation* *Hobbies e.g. craft work, **writing*** *Seeing grandchildren*
NOT IMPORTANT	*Answering the phone* *Answering the door*	*Checking emails regularly* *Watching daytime TV* *Window shopping*

1. Now find 3 activities you could cut out of your own NOT URGENT - NOT IMPORTANT square so that you have

more time for those in the Golden Square, including writing.

Writers use different techniques to help them complete their work, and one of these may suit you:

- Pick a regular time each day or week and stick to it
- Plan out periods when you know you can work undisturbed and keep to a definite timetable
- Try to write *something* for five minutes every day, whether you want to or not. You will usually find that you then change your mind and want to continue.
- Work on a more ad hoc basis, as and when ideas come to you, if this has proved in the past to be the right way for you to work. Monitor yourself carefully in case it turns out to be an excuse not to write.

Writing things down

Activity 5

Memories are not orderly, but appear out of the blue when you hear, see, smell, taste or touch something that takes you back in time. Buy yourself a notebook and start taking it everywhere you go. Use it to jot down any thoughts or ideas you have at the moment they arrive.

For your main body of work, writing with a pen in long hand appeals to many people. If you prefer to work this way, make sure your writing is legible to you (when you read it back later) and to anyone who may be helping you compile your material.

A word of warning – don't buy beautifully hard-bound journals unless you are prepared to copy out the material again later. If you keep your material loose-leaf e.g. in a folder or box file, and write on separate pieces of paper or in spiral-bound pads where you can tear sheets out, it will mean that as extra memories of particular times come back and you write them down, or you decide to reorganise your work, you can slip new written pieces into the right place alongside other material covering the same period. For some people, speaking into a tape recorder may be another helpful way to get ideas down fast and you can then write them out at your leisure.

Computers are ideal for autobiography as you can cut and paste chunks of work, will always have copies, everything is 100% readable and you can send off professional-looking material to possible publishers very easily. But you can manage without if you do not own or enjoy using a computer.

Conclusion
You should now have a better understanding of why you are working through this book, how you are going to manage the time and place to write and what sort of self-imposed barriers/stumbling blocks you may need to watch out for.

And now try this...........

Here is the first writing exercise to get you started. Do NOT worry at this stage about your writing style, mistakes in grammar or anything else, but just write as if you are talking to a friend.

Who are you?

Your autobiography is all about you, so we are going to start by exploring something that can be a sensitive and personal issue – your name. The exercise should also help you get in touch with your feelings, which is another important part of any good writing.

    a. Where does your name come from?

    b. What do you feel about it?

    c. Write a few paragraphs about one memory you have concerning your name. For example, did it cause you any specific problem, did something funny happen that relates to it or were you given a special nickname that you can write about?

Make a note of any other memories this exercise evokes and the period in your life the various memories relate to. You may find you want to keep them and use them later in your finished work.

****

Chapter 2 - The Time Line

Introduction

Although it is not essential to write your autobiography in exact chronological or date order, one of the most helpful techniques when starting to write a life history is to create a time line. This is simply an annotated list or picture of your life from birth to the present day. It allows you to start planning out your autobiography without having to remember any of the personal 'bits' or a great amount of detail. This is because the starting point is factual information that should be readily available.

Dividing up the time line

I have found that the best way to set out the information is to do it in small chunks of time that are all of equal length. Instead of noting down every single year of your life, I suggest that you divide your age roughly by 6, so that you end up with six separate sections.

If you are 75, this will mean your six sections each contain 12 or 13 years and so your time line could cover the following periods:

1. 0 – 12
2. 13 – 24
3. 25 – 36
4. 37 – 48
5. 49 – 60
6. 61 - now

If you are 44, your six sections will look like this:

1. 0 – 7
2. 8 – 14
3. 15 – 21
4. 22 – 28
5. 29 – 35
6. 36 – now

As well as your age in years, events in the past are often associated with the actual year they took place, so add years for each section e.g. 0 – 12, 1947 – 1959.

Activity 1

Note down the six sections that suit your own age best. Next to the years, add the actual dates.

How to write a time line

Although called a time line, you don't have to literally draw a line – although you can if you want to. What you will be doing is adding in events, experiences, anniversaries, people around at the time, special occasions, operations, crises etc to your six sections to build up a factual picture of your past life. This is a fairly long-term project as new events and small details will occur to you at odd moments as you go about your life or work on other aspects of your autobiography. Because you will continually remember new facts that need to be added in, it is important to give yourself lots of room.

My preference is for six loose pieces of paper, each with the appropriate years and ages for that section set out as a single heading. You then have the whole sheet for noting down the events that took place during that time period and can add a second or third sheet later as more details come back to you.

Some people like to see it all on one page and even have it on the wall, and so prefer to draw a line along the bottom or down the side of a large sheet of paper, or unroll a sheet of lining paper and draw the time line on that. The only disadvantage is that you will probably run out of room for particular sections and will have to find a way to splice in extra paper.

Getting started
Armed with your six sections, it is time to get down the known information, major events or activities associated with each time period. Here are some ideas of what you will find it easy to pinpoint and put down, as the dates are usually fairly accessible:

Births – your brothers and sisters, nephews and nieces, cousins, friends or more distant family members whose life impinged on your own. The births of your own children, grandchildren or great grandchildren.

Deaths – parents, grandparents, siblings, your own children or grandchildren, husbands or partners and the deaths of friends, relatives or colleagues that affected you.

Marriages and divorces – again, your own or those of people around you such as step-parents, grandparents, your children or aunts and uncles.

*

Activity 2

Add at least 5 different births, marriages or deaths to your time line.

Places

You can now start jotting down all the information associated with where you were living. Even if the exact dates are not clear, you will know where you lived when you were brought into the world and can probably identify the general age you were when you moved from your first home. Most people move several times in their lives and so you can now add all the other homes you had such as your first married home, army quarters, boarding school, university digs, nurses' or other work quarters and temporary hostels or beds-its. You could also note down when you moved in to the home that you live in now.

Institutions

Once you start noting down homes, you will probably remember the schools, colleges, university, work and other institutions or establishments that you joined in your lifetime and again should be able to note them down in the correct sections of your time line.

General events

Now that you get the idea of facts related to years or ages, you will be able to really start filling in the six sections. There are so many aspects that will be personal to your own life that it is hard to give examples, but they could include anything from going to live on a farm to joining up, getting promoted, training to be a

28

pilot, performing your first solo as a violinist, becoming self-employed or moving abroad. Put them down in the right section and you will find your time line is starting to build into quite a large body of work.

Activity 3

For one of your six periods, write down 7 or 8 known facts, major events or aspects of life which you were involved in or that you know affected you.

Here is an example in my own life for one 10-year period:

- Moving from London to the West Country
- Getting married
- Having two children
- Training to be a teacher
- Setting up my own business
- Moving to Central England
- Specialising in teaching computing to adults.

Feelings

It is most likely that, as you note down one or two factual events such as a marriage or a new house, you will feel quite strong emotions. Perhaps the event was a joyous one, or remembering it makes you sad or angry.

It is very important that, if an autobiography is to be meaningful for the writer and for your readers, it is NOT simply a list of events but includes your emotions, views and reasons for any choices you made. Later on as you work through this book you will have lots of time to explore some of the events you are listing now in much greater depth, but if you want to do so straight away, it is a good idea to start on a new piece of paper and simply write down as much as you can about the particular event that has stirred your memory.

<u>Writing it down</u>

As this book is about writing as well as remembering, it is never too early to start a piece of written work. So, after any attempt at remembering something in your past, you should be prepared to write about it. When you do this:

- Don't worry about the actual writing skills. Write as if you are telling a story or speaking to a friend.

- Try to think back to that period of time or to the activities you are describing and draw a picture that includes as much detail as possible. This should include feelings, views and emotions as well as the facts themselves.

- Add a note at the bottom of your piece to include the dates your story refers to, or your age at the time, and the general theme on which you are writing. This will help you slot it in to the correct period or section when you eventually put all the pieces of writing together.

Activity 4

Take any topic at all from your time line and write something about it in the form of a short scene, using the tips listed above.

Spidergrams

Having identified many events or activities by linking them to periods of your life, you may need help in remembering them in more detail. One method which is particularly successful for people who remember pictorially is the spidergram.

This is a device that is also used in essay writing or planning a project as it is a way of generating new ideas that relate to an original topic or theme.

(Tony Buzan has published books about a very similar technique that he calls 'mind maps'.)

To create a spidergram, write the major event in the centre of a blank piece of paper and start to daydream or think back to that time. When a thought arrives in your head, write it down and draw a line linking it to the central idea. If it takes you off down a particular path, keep noting down events or ideas and link each one with a line to the topic that triggered the thought. When you get to a dead end, go back to the central idea and take off in a new direction. You will eventually fill the page with a number of linked memories, events or activities related to the central theme.

You will see that when your paper is covered in lines and notes it looks rather like a spider's web, which is how the technique got its name.

Spidergrams should not be confused with brainstorming because that involves putting down any ideas that come to you without analysing them or making connections.

Example spidergram.

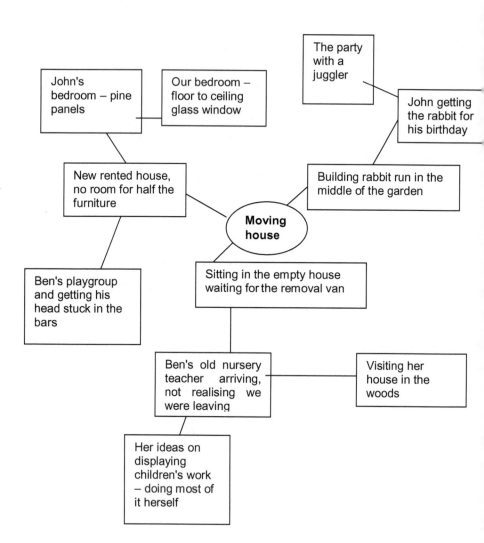

Activity 5

Take any event from your time line and have a go at creating a spidergram.

Conclusion

This is the start of an on-going piece of work – completing as much as you can of your time line – and the time you spend on it is crucial to you succeeding in completing your autobiography. It is therefore something that you should keep coming back to in between working on the other chapters in this book. It will act as the peg on which to hang all your stories and will help you generate the data around which your finished manuscript will be based.

Even if you ignore or leave out half of the memories in the end, having identified the key events in your life will be of great help when you come to later chapters that concentrate on organising your material. You will be able to see which are the full and which are the thin areas of your remembered life and identify the topics or events that you want to include in your finished piece of work.

And now try this....

1. Go back to a period in your time line that you have not yet fully annotated and make a list of 5 or 6 significant events or experiences from that time. Add as many details as you want to.

2. For one of the events, draw as full a spidergram as you can.

3. For one of the memories that this generates, write a short piece about it. This can either be purely descriptive or you can make it into a little story.

It is also time to start reading as many autobiographies as you can. There are hundreds of such books in libraries or bookshops that show the many different ways that others have tackled writing their autobiography. They should generate lots of ideas for how to organise and present your own work.

* * * * * * * * * * *

Chapter 3-Memory Joggers:-Informal Methods

Introduction

One of the main stumbling blocks to writing an autobiography is a general lack of memories, or the difficulty we all have as we get older in remembering enough details to make a particular time period worth writing about. Yet once you find the right trigger, the floodgates can suddenly open and you will hopefully be remembering things you haven't thought about for years and years.

For some parts of your life, even very far back in the past, you will have vivid memories. Perhaps it was your first visit to the dentist, a particular day out, a friend's new hairstyle or the lurid details of that squalid bed-sit you rented as a student. Whatever the memory, something will have triggered it so that you are now able to recall it in great detail. Identifying techniques that will help you remember more of your past is the aim of this and the next chapter.

Ways people remember

We all know that people learn in different ways, and that is why you are often unsuccessful on one educational course – perhaps one that relies heavily on demonstrations or watching videos – and yet very good on another that is more practically based, aimed at those who prefer to learn through 'doing'.

Just like learning, we remember in different ways, and you may find you recall events more easily using one of these methods:

- Through words – reading, writing and discussion
- Pictorially
- Kinaesthetically – physically, through touch or handling concrete objects

So far this book has introduced three different techniques for helping you go back in time:

- thinking about your name
- drawing and annotating a time line
- (More pictorially) creating a spidergram.

In this chapter, I am going to introduce four more quite different techniques that you can try that relate to the different remembering styles.

<u>Life Coaching Techniques</u>

Life coaching is about helping and encouraging people to move forward in their lives. Here are two techniques used by life coaches that may help you to remember the past.

Wheel of life

This technique in life coaching has two aims:

- To help people take stock of how satisfied they are with particular areas of their life
- To identify ways of redressing any imbalance.

So, for example, by rating different areas they might discover that they are very satisfied with their working life but want to change an unsatisfactory relationship or do something about their health and fitness.

For an autobiography, instead of concentrating on satisfactions or balance, you can use the same techniques to help recall happy, sad, funny or disturbing incidents that took place within these same areas of life.

The Wheel of Life works best as a pictorial memory jogger where you are going to divide your life into 'pie sectors' – but you could create a list as an alternative if you prefer.

Firstly, you need to come up with between 7 and 10 different headings or categories under which you would like to describe the meaningful areas of your life. For example, here are a few that you may find helpful and you can add or substitute your own headings:

1. Finance
2. Health and fitness
3. Environment (or Home)
4. Work
5. Family
6. Relationships
7. Politics
8. Spiritual life
9. Leisure and relaxation
10. Friendship
11. Intellectual development
12. Contribution to society

Now draw a circle, divide it into the same number of segments as the categories you have come up with and write the name of the category in each segment. It will look something like this.

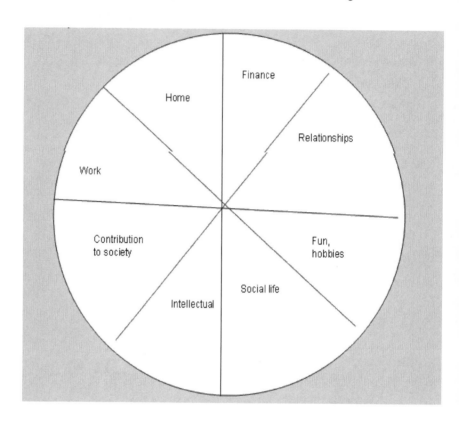

Activity 1

Draw your own wheel.

To help jog your memory, you could first rate your current satisfactions within each segment. For example, out of 10, how many would you give your financial position, health or social life?

To see this take shape, mark your rating in the pie sector along an imaginary line between the centre and the margin, and then join up the marks round the circle. You will get a wavy line and quickly see the high and low areas of your life at the present time.

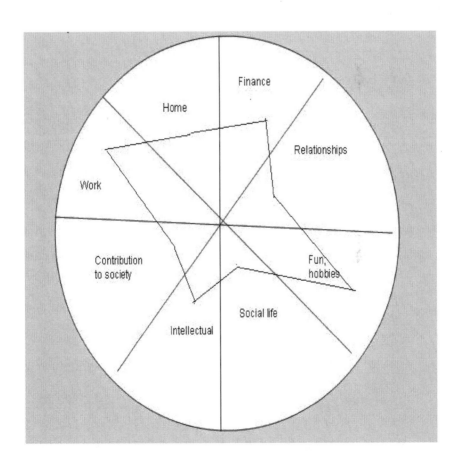

If you have given any category a low rating, can you remember a time when you were in a better position? For example, if you rated your health as low, when were you at your healthiest?

Now, do the opposite and think about a time when you would have rated that area of life much lower than you do now.

Finally, thinking about just one of the categories, can you remember in some detail any incident that took place in the past related to that topic? Jot down a few notes to remind yourself of what happened.

Activity 2

Take any category and remember an incident or activity:
  1. List five things you remember enjoying about it
  2. List five things you remember disliking about it

As a means of jogging your memory the ideal is to come up with as many examples as possible taken from your past. Your categories could even be re-labelled so that they are *previous* homes, *times of poverty or riches, former* relationships, *past* holidays or *old* friends.

Here is an example from my past:

Friendships and social life – some of my happiest memories are of my time in a university hall of residence when I had a close circle of girlfriends all studying similar subjects. I also remember feeling part of a 'family' when I worked as a careers adviser in London, as we worked in our local colleges for most of the week but met up every Friday at the central office for meetings, lunch and a good chat.

Activity 3

Take one of your categories and write up a story about a pleasurable, funny or sad memory associated with it. Try to remember as much detail as you can about the people, places or events you are describing.

Roles we play

A very different life coaching technique is to think of your life in terms of the roles you play, in order to work on improving your satisfaction in them. This is much wider than just the official roles you might hold such as Manager, Secretary or Technician as it also covers family, home, community and other roles. To help jog your memory, you need to think back to all the roles you have ever played.

Here are just a few examples of unofficial, relationship or unpaid roles:

Father
Daughter
Brother
Wife
Grandmother
Nephew
Cook (for the family)
Health visitor (when relatives are ill)

Protester
Committee member
Teacher (helping with homework)
Volunteer
Hairdresser (cutting partner's hair)
Fundraiser
Driver (to take children to school)
Financier (handling the family budget)
Gardner

Activity 4

Spend 5 minutes writing down as many roles as you can think of that you have ever held in your life. You may well come up with 50 – 100.

As soon as you start imagining yourself *in* a role, I am sure you will be able to think of events that took place that you might otherwise have forgotten. For example, what can you remember happened to you when you were being a brother or sister, an aunt or a grandfather?

Just taking the role of parent, do you remember, for example, what it felt like when you were caring for a baby as a new mum or dad? Did you ever take your toddler shopping and 'lose' them, or did they embarrass you in the supermarket queue? Can you recall a time when you shared a storybook with a child, gave them a bath, decorated a bedroom or made clothes for them and something happened as a result of that? Or what about when you tried to discipline a wayward teenager or your 21 year-old turned up on the doorstep with no-where to live?

Activity 5

Choose any role and write a short piece describing something that happened when you were in that role. Try to get in touch with the feelings you had, as well as the facts about the incident. Can you remember if it changed you in any way?

<u>Lists</u>

A common practice in primary schools used to be to ask children to write essays around the theme of "*My favourite........*" E.g. *holiday, meal, pet, relative* etc. Well, this technique works even better for an autobiographical writer as the first thing to do before being able to decide what to write about is to list all the items from which to choose your favourite.

You can make lists of almost anything and immediately you will start remembering people, places or events. Here are a few topics to start off a list:

- Countries I have visited
- Houses I have lived in
- Pets
- Friends
- Sporting events
- Scents
- Meals
- Restaurants
- Celebrities I have met
- Clothes
- Favourite rooms

- Games
- Celebrations
- Hospitals I have stayed in
- Cars I have owned
- Favourite flowers or plants
- Schools
- Holidays

Activity 6

Think of 10 different topics that could form the basis of a meaningful list in your own life.

Once you have a topic, you can start noting down all the items that make up your list. These could either be in chronological or date order, or they may just pop into your head in a higgledy piggledy way.

So for example, if you have chosen *Countries I have visited*, it is probably quickest just to jot down any country you can think of and, if it turns out to be necessary, re-order the list by date when it is complete. On the other hand, to make a list of *homes* you may find it easier to tie the exercise up with your time line.

To help even more, you may evoke the memories through your senses e.g. cook the meals, re-visit some of the places or smell the flowers or perfumes (e.g. in a garden centre or a department store).

*

Activity 7

1. Take one topic and make a full list.

2. Now take just one item on the list and write up a sketch or story related to it.

As an example of holidays, I have a vivid memory of spending time in France with my father when I was about eight. An octopus caught by one of his friends was beaten against the rocks to kill it for lunch.

When it comes to celebrities I have met: I once had a brief encounter with a well-known celebrity in a café in Tottenham Court Road. Straight off the train and dying to visit the loo, I first bought a coffee but didn't want to leave it on the table where it might be cleared away. I approached a middle-aged woman sitting with her own drink and piece of cake and asked her to mind my cup. She was faintly surprised but agreed, and as she looked up I realised it was Victoria Wood. Being well behaved, I pretended I didn't recognise her and after returning to collect the cup, simply smiled my thanks and sat at a different table. I kept hoping she would write this small incident into a sketch – but she never did.

Memorabilia

The final method is one for kinaesthetic remembering as it is all about objects that you can touch.

We all know that photographs are a brilliant memory device – although it is quite easy to imagine you remember when you are in fact simply absorbing the picture in front of you – but there are hundreds of different objects that can also evoke memories.

Activity 8

Name 5 different **types** of object that you have in your home – including those in the loft, garden or garage - that will have memories attached.

Some examples you may have listed include:

- Books
- Toys
- Letters and cards
- Paintings
- Diaries
- Clothes, including hats and shoes
- Jewellery
- Keys
- Tickets or programmes
- Ornaments
- Furniture
- Lamps
- Cooking or gardening equipment
- Radios and TVs
- Holiday souvenirs
- School reports and certificates

> **Activity 9**
>
> Look round your home and find an object, handle it (even smell it or put it on!) and then write a story from the past about it.

As an on-going activity, you may like to start collecting various memorabilia together in a box or in your workroom. You will then have them to hand and can use them to help you get in touch with past experiences you want to include in your autobiography.

On one of my courses, several members brought in photos and letters and one showed us an old oil lamp used to light her way to bed in rural England. To me, the most interesting object was the book "Shakespeare Wallah" brought in by someone who recalled a visit by Felicity Kendall's family touring company of actors to her school in India in the 1950s.

Music

Although not an object you can handle, a piece of music such as a song or symphony can evoke very strong memories, and so it seems most appropriate to slot it in with memorabilia that you can see, touch, taste and smell as it makes up the fifth sense.

When looking round the house, in the garage or up in the attic for items to prompt your memories, don't forget to play a record or download a soundtrack as this may be just as valuable as putting on an old pair of shoes or handling a favourite children's book.

Conclusion

Once you have discovered a successful method for jogging your memory, or if you particularly enjoyed any of these techniques, continue using it to build up more material for your portfolio.

And now try this.......

Using any of the techniques covered in this chapter, take one *new* category from life, role you have played, list item OR object/sound that so far you have not written about. Write a short story, sketch or descriptive piece about it.

* * * * * * * * * * *

Chapter 4-Memory Joggers: -Formal Methods

Introduction

Whatever method you use for jogging your memory, as long as it encourages you to go back in time and remember past events in enough detail it should be valued and practised regularly as it means it is an effective technique for helping you write about your life. No one method will work for everyone but I hope you have been pleasantly surprised by the success you have had with at least one of the methods covered so far.

The difference between the methods outlined earlier and those in this chapter are fairly arbitrary, but you could say that as all three of the techniques we are now going to cover relate in some way to printed documents, they could be seen as more 'formal' methods.

The CV

Whether or not you have applied for any jobs recently - or plan to do so in the near future - the Curriculum Vitae or CV is a goldmine for an autobiographer. If you do not have an old copy you could update easily, or if you have never created one in your life before, it is definitely worth drawing one up. That is because this is a document that concentrates in a very specific way on three major areas of life:

- Education and training
- Work – both paid and unpaid
- Achievements

If you do not have a CV, you will need to get down the details, although using simple note form is fine if you won't be using it to apply for work.

For many people, one of the major self-imposed barriers to writing an autobiography is a fear of being boring, or not having done much in life to be proud of. For example, if you have had an erratic or limited work history, it may be painful to address it now. However, the final decision about what to include in the finished manuscript is yours. You may discover that, looking back on what you once regarded as a black area or low point can throw up some valuable lessons or important details that may contribute to your story when you finally write about your life.

Education and training

You normally create an education and training section on a CV that includes information about the secondary schools, colleges, university or other institutions you have ever attended, examinations passed, the courses you took - including in-house training - any roles you held, prizes or awards and other extra-curricular activities you undertook during your school or college days such as membership of clubs, scouts etc.

For example:

1957 – 64   Settington Comprehensive School, Colesworthy
GCSEs: 7 including Maths, English and French
            Studied Textiles for two years
            Awarded Marshall Prize for Art in the Community –
            poster chosen to publicise a new Community
            Centre

Activity 1

Find an old CV or start writing a new one so that you have an education and training section to draw on.

Looking at this area of your life should help you start thinking back and remembering the years when you were at school or college or in some form of training.

During those times, many things must have happened to you. Some ideas of what might be relevant in your own life and what you could focus on include:

- Getting into trouble at school
- Special friendships
- Failing or succeeding at particular subjects
- A teacher you particularly liked or disliked
- An incident e.g. concerning a school pet, lab experiment, item of woodwork equipment or school play
- A romance on a training course
- Bonding or team development games
- Your first year at university

Activity 2

Take one period or incident that has come into your mind and write something about it. Make sure it is clear from the context what age you were, where the event took place and how it affected you.

Employment and other work

The other main section of a CV involves all those jobs you will have had. These could be for named employers, for small concerns, as a temp, running your own business, working freelance, acting as a volunteer, working as an apprentice or even spending a few weeks on work experience.

Just because some work may have been unpaid, short term or temporary does not make it any less valuable as far as the development of skills, building relationships or general experience are concerned and so it is important to have the details available for all the work experience you have ever had. (You will find that it is the little details that help more than anything to bring your story to life.)

One tricky area when it comes to applying for jobs is if you are asked to explain the reasons for leaving your previous places of employment. However, for your life story this can be another extremely valuable piece of information!

For a CV, and even more for an autobiography, the important aspects of work experience include tasks and responsibilities. Rather than just noting down your job title and the name of the employer, it is very important to look back at the work and include the particular activities you were engaged in. In this way the job is more likely to come alive and you will be able to remember far more. So, if you have a CV that is just a list of dates and titles, go back and add more "......**ing**" words in the description.

For example, instead of noting that you were an Administrator for the Cotswold Training Company, you might want to include the fact that you were involved in: *"organising training schedules, booking student places, handling payments and acting as the first point of contact for tutors."* If you haven't written a CV before, your work experience is usually set out in just the same way as your education and training. For example:

1975 – 78   Hamilton Business Centre, Dymchurch
             P.A. to Centre Manager – *making appointments, organising conferences and meetings and booking space at the Centre*

1979 – 82   Cotswold Training Centre
             Administrator - *organising training schedules, booking student places, handling payments and acting as the first point of contact for tutors*

Caring or bringing up a family
Some of you may have been looking after a relative or bringing up a family for all or most of your working life and may feel rather left out of this section. However, not only will you be writing about this side of life in your autobiography – you were probably doing much more than you think during this time.

For example, full time mothers are often involved in all sorts of community activities from acting as parent helpers at playgroup or school, making school clothes or costumes, organising the school run or walk-to-school sessions or helping teach cycling or swimming.

Whatever your major role, you may also be involved in activities unrelated to children or caring such as selling handmade cards or other crafts, such as making cakes for jumble sales.

These are all activities that should go down on a CV and so use one of these examples to write about if you cannot find any work-related memories.

Activity 3

Once you have found (or written) the work experience part of a CV, take one of the earliest job entries and think back to that time. Write a brief description of your workplace, some of the tasks you had to perform and any particularly memorable incidents.

Achievements

Although not in a separate section, a CV is the chance to promote yourself and show yourself in the best possible light. So when applying for jobs, most people use every opportunity to provide evidence (not empty boasting) that they achieved something during any particular time.

For an autobiography, it is equally important to remember the successes. If you find this hard, ask yourself the following question:

What am I most proud of about my time at ....?

Success can be tangible and concrete e.g. sold more ......, was promoted to ...., built the first .... ran a successful ....

Success can also be emotional and hard to define, but it could involve overcoming a fear, identifying a strength you didn't know you had or making a contribution to society.

For example:

- Living on my own for the first time, learning to cook and look after the flat
- Passing my driving test after several failed attempts, so that I could get the job
- Overcoming initial hostility from my boss and becoming good friends

---

Activity 4

Think back to a period of your work or time in education and remember and then write about something you are particularly proud of.

Family Tree

Although this is not a book about genealogy, your relatives are clearly a vital part of your own story. In particular, there are those whom you would actually have met and related to and also those distant ones who may have influenced your life in some way.

Activity 5

Sketch out as much of your family tree as you can remember on a large piece of paper. It usually helps to identify the generations if you draw it up in the form of a hierarchy of different levels.

Don't worry at this stage if some names slip your mind as this is easily remedied with a little research. Over the next few days or weeks, carry on working on your sketch. For each person in the tree, think back to any times you met or were in contact with them and start noting down memories about those times next to their names.

Now think about the relatives you never met because they live too far away or they have died and see if you can find a definite connection with any of them.

For example:

Did you inherit a particular trait or skill you could explore?

- o Did they influence your parents or give advice that affected your own life?
- o Did they leave anything to you or a relative in their will that changed your own life in some way?
- o Were you ever compared to them?

Activity 6

1. Take one relative who has some connection to you and write a character sketch about them that clearly shows what they were like. As well as their physical appearance, try to show their character in their actions.

2. What would be the reason for including them in your own life story?

Maps

A pictorial memory jogger that works extremely well for some people is to draw maps of places that meant something to you. These could be your childhood home, your first married rented flat, a holiday cottage and nearby town or digs when you had your first acting job.

Once you have added as much detail as possible – and you can include little stick figures if that helps you – you will need to "walk" round it either by moving your fingers along the roads or just in your mind. Each time you come to a landmark such as a bus stop or doctor's surgery, you will find yourself remembering events that took place there.

Start this exercise by thinking of a time you would really like to remember more about but find quite hard to do so.

Activity 7

1. Draw a map of where you were living - the houses, streets, bus stops, neighbouring houses, railway station, shops or anything else that was close by. Where possible, write the names of everyone and everything e.g. your neighbours, the streets, the cinema or the dentist in the appropriate place.

2. Move round physically or in your mind until you start to remember.

3. Write a story about one event that took place or memory that comes to mind.

If you find after trying to carry out this activity for one place that you come to a dead end, you can use a real map to help fill in the gaps in your memory.

For every place you have lived, worked or visited there will be a map. Nowadays, *Google maps* (go to www.google.co.uk and click the Maps link) will allow you to type in a town or postcode and zoom in on the streets and motorways as well as the general terrain and even the actual buildings, or you can turn to more conventional Ordinance Survey or town maps available from a library, tourist office or shop.

If you were there a long time ago, bear in mind that things may have changed and certain streets and buildings may have been altered or could even be gone forever.

Conclusion

The last two chapters have been an attempt to find as many ways as possible to help you remember the past, so that you can fill in all the gaps there will naturally be in your memories. However, it is important that you do not see these exercises as the end of your work but only the beginning.

Use any memory jogging methods that work for you to cover the years on your time line (or any other method you choose) to write as many descriptions, stories, sketches and anecdotes as you can that come to mind. The aim is to produce more than enough material to draw on when you start organising and pairing it all down to the finished product.

This is the end of the memory jogging part of the book but if you think of any other methods that might take you back in time, use them to write up some more memories.

There is one more method to come that serves two different purposes and this will be introduced in Chapter 6.

And now try this...........

Either use your CV, family tree or a map to remind yourself of someone from the past you have not written about and relate a story about your dealings with them.

* * * * * * * * * * *

Chapter 5 - Bringing Your Writing to Life

Introduction

So far, the most important thing has been to get down as much as you can of remembered details before your memories lose their freshness and begin to fade. This means that, although some of the memories will be in the form of proper stories, many others will still be rough notes. But it has been more important to write it down than to worry about how it is written.

If you want other people to enjoy reading your life story, you obviously need to do more than just get down the basic facts. So this chapter will look at a number of different techniques you can use to help improve those first drafts.

Clarity

Everything you write will be crystal clear to you personally, as you will be describing events that you have witnessed. But unless you are very careful, and especially if you introduce a large cast or have a lot of ground to cover and choose to move backwards and forwards in time, your readers may not be fully in the picture and may become confused. (If you have ever read a book where you suddenly find yourself wondering who is talking, or when an event took place, you will know what I mean!)

The only way to prevent confusion arising is to check that, at least implicitly, you have included as much as you can of the following information:

Who is this part about? When you first mention someone by name or introduce a new character, think about whether their role or relationships are clear. If not, try to think of a way to introduce them to readers so that they are aware of the person's significance to the story or why they have been introduced.

What is going on? A common mistake made by autobiographers is to overwhelm their readers with too much detail because they cannot bear to leave anything out. If you realise this and try to cut back some of the material, there is a danger that you'll go too far the other way. (This is often the case when a film is made from a book and the audience literally lose the plot.) Ideally, make sure that readers are given enough information to understand exactly what is happening but don't give them more than is necessary.

Why is something included, or why was a particular decision made? A straightforward descriptive piece may not need reasons, but in part of your autobiography it can be important for readers to understand exactly why something happened. For example, there may be a particular point you want to make or a lesson to be learned. If this is the case, you don't want it obscured.

Where did an event take place? Not many life stories are limited to one location or geographical area and so each time you write a new scene, check that your readers will know where everything is taking place if it is an important aspect of the story. Also remember that the setting for any scene can be very important, so include small details that will show this clearly.

When did an event take place? It is easy to forget that if your work covers a lengthy period of time, your readers could end up confused as to where they are in the story. In particular, it can be very irritating if it isn't clear that an important event took place *before* you moved or *after* the baby was born, or whether you were a teenager or grandfather at that particular time. Obviously you won't want to mention ages and dates every chapter, but if your readers need to know when an event took place, make sure you include these facts somewhere.

How did it come about? If your writing is good, your readers will hopefully be intrigued and this means they will be asking themselves "How" questions – How did it get broken? How did he get out of the camp? How did she look when you met her again? Even if you only want to answer these questions bit-by-bit or later in the story, make sure they ARE answered and your readers are not left frustrated and unsatisfied.

Activity 1

Either work on a piece you have already written and revise it, or take any memory and write about it. Check that the who, what, why, where, when and how questions are all answered.

Hidden meanings

As you look back at the past, you often see significance that was lost to you at the time, and so the whole exercise of writing an autobiography is likely to throw up some fascinating insights. However, it doesn't make them any easier to write about and it is quite possible that, in some of your writing, if you get very involved perhaps when describing the surroundings or appearance of people - the true significance will be lost.

The following activity shows how to check that you have not lost sight of the real point of the piece.

Imagine you have written a short story about visiting your grandmother as a small boy, and the food and drink is lovingly described. If you now just note down four or five key words or phrases that sum up the event, these could be: visit granny, cake, spilled drink, cross, hitting.

If visiting granny and her getting cross actually happened on other occasions too, you may possibly want to rewrite your story to place more emphasis on this side of her character.

Activity 2
1. Take any piece of writing that you believe is fairly clear.
2. Read through and note down the four or five key words that you believe sum it up.
3. Is a darker moment, lesson to be learned or hidden meaning exposed? If so, re-write the piece to bring this out.

The five senses

Having delved into your memories and drawn out the details of a particular event or experience, it should be straightforward to write down the basic facts. But making your scenes vivid and colourful is a different task.

You will already have discovered that memories can be triggered by something that happens to you in the present time, which is why I suggested in Chapter 1 that you keep a notebook with you at all times.

Here are some examples:

- The sound of a bell may bring back memories of school days, factory work, living near a church or even war- time.
- The touch of velvet may remind you of a party dress you once wore or the curtains that hung in a former dining room.
- The smell of fresh coffee or cakes baking may evoke thoughts of family meals, mother's baking days, restaurant visits or French holidays.
- The taste of Guinness always reminds me of my grandfather when I was small as he used to let me have a sip of his beer whenever I visited him.
- The sight of a dog lead can trigger thoughts of your own pets, walks in the park or life in the country.

As we have such a strong response to sounds, tastes, textures and smells as well as things we see, you will find that where your writing involves more of the five senses it will have a greater impact on your readers than a visual description alone. They will smell the smells, hear the sounds and taste the same tastes – and the piece of writing will come alive.

*

Activity 3

1. Pick any event from the past.

2. Write about 100 words describing it, making sure you introduce at least two or three different senses.

3. Now find a piece of descriptive writing you have completed and see if you can add in an extra sense.

As an example of the use of sound in writing, here is an excerpt from my grandfather's autobiography:

"What I liked best was to hear the womenfolk singing as they returned home after their days work in the fields, particularly in July and August.. No Russian could ever forget their singing as it was always the same tune sung in a very high key, but one could only hear their song when they were away in the distance. It was a mystery to me, but when I grew older I found out that as soon as they saw someone approaching they would stop singing. When they passed you, sometimes in a party of six, or ten or even twenty, you would ask yourself if it was these women you had heard singing as they would be just walking silently along, most of them carrying a parcel of grass, flowers or sometimes straw, and each one carrying a scythe."

Similes and Metaphors

There are two figures of speech that fiction writers are always encouraged to include in their work and which are equally valid for an autobiographer to use. These are similes and metaphors.

The reason for using them is that they create an image in the mind of the reader far more effectively than plain description

66

and very often will save you having to describe something in any detail at all. In particular, they can encourage people to visualize objects or understand concepts that may be abstract and difficult to describe, by evoking a more familiar picture or experience.

The key to successfully including them in your writing is to try and avoid using too many of the really boring clichés (over-worn phrases that we all instantly recognise) and to use them sparingly, with care. The best writers introduce them in fresh and imaginative ways but even if you cannot create your own, the odd well-known phrase can still lift a piece of writing and make it livelier and more memorable.

Similes

These involve comparing two dissimilar things that have one key aspect in common. (The more outrageous the difference between the objects, the more exciting these can be.) The joining words are usually **as......as**, **than** or **like.**

For example:

- The meringue was as light as a cloud
- His socks smelled like ripe cheese
- She was as prickly as a little cat
- My fingers were so cold they felt like icicles
- He was happier than King Canute when the tide turned.

*

Activity 4

1. Create similes for the following ideas:
   - My marriage is ....
   - The weather was ....
   - He coughed ....
2. Look back at any descriptive piece you have written and try to rewrite a part to include a simile.

Metaphors

These involve understanding one thing in terms of another (as if it actually IS something else) rather than using the words *as* or *like*. They are harder to employ but can be even more exciting in a piece of writing.

For example:
- The plate was filled with clouds of meringue
- He was burning with anger
- That year, a whole new crop of trainees joined my department

"She felt she could tell right from wrong only because she had been repeatedly informed of the difference; her opinions were twitching, vulnerable tadpoles compared with the honking frogs that were her parents' views" - Julian Barnes "Staring at the Sun"

Here are the steps to take to create your own metaphors:
  1. Decide on the subject or idea you want to write about

2. Identify the emotion you want to evoke such as its beauty, its speed, how frightening it was or how much joy it brought.
3. Think of a separate object or idea that is normally regarded as being beautiful, frightening, fast or bringing joy.
4. Put the two together.

So if a *train journey* is your subject you may want to convey its *speed*. Bullets and arrows both go fast and so you could combine the two images and write about a train journey where "....the train was released from the station and shot towards its target."

Mixed metaphors - where two different and often conflicting images are evoked to describe the same concept - are to be avoided if possible as they are usually quite ridiculous.
For example: *He shot the wind out of her saddle* (rather than sails).

Activity 5

Choose 3 from the following list of ideas or objects and create a metaphor for each one:

- A funeral
- Sitting an exam
- Giving a speech
- A pet
- A long awaited phone call
- My computer
- My favourite room

Conflict, drama and emotion

It has been said that *"conflict is the momentum for change"*. If you examine a gripping piece of writing you are likely to find that it is the conflict, drama or deep emotions in the story that make you want to keep reading, rather than any descriptive detail or general account of events. The whole point of introducing these sorts of "dramas" into your own writing is to make sure your writing isn't flat and one-dimensional.

Of greatest interest in an autobiography is how you dealt with any conflict and coped when things went wrong; what the final outcome was and in what way it may have changed you or your life.

There are various types of conflict that you can introduce into your story and these include:

- Inner conflict, where you had to fight your own demons or weaknesses e.g. greed, pride, laziness or fear

- A fight with nature where you were battling physically or faced a dangerous situation e.g. extremes of weather such as heat waves or floods or an encounter with wild animals

- A protagonist who was particularly trying or hoping to force you to do something you didn't want to do such as a bullying employer, mad relative, irate customer or "authority" e.g. the law or council officials

- Problems with inanimate objects such as farm machinery or a bath hoist

- Constraints such as time, work deadlines or finding a baby sitter
- Relationship problems

Activity 6

Look back over your time line or think back to a particular period in your life and note down two or three definite conflicts – internal or external – that you could write about.

Turning points

Related to conflict but perhaps less dramatic is the idea of turning points. If you don't see your story as one full of drama and heated emotion, you will still find that you had to make certain decisions, or changes were forced on you by circumstances, and these will have led you in a different direction. Occasionally such changes can be so fundamental that you almost become a new person. These points are some of the most interesting and important in your life story and so you need to make sure you emphasise them rather than ignore or gloss over them.

For example:

-   You didn't get that job – what difference did it make and how differently did your life turn out?
-   You turned down a proposal from one person – how would life have turned out if you had made a different decision?
-   You couldn't have the children you wanted, what did that make you do instead?

- You had a car accident and had to stop playing professional rugby –how did you react?

Activity 7

Think of any decision you have made, or change of circumstances that was forced upon you, write something about it and explain how this led you in a different direction.

Suspense

How many times do you start a book and then realise it is so uninspiring, you can't be bothered to finish it? To make sure no-one views your autobiography in the same way, you need to make readers want more. A simple way to do this is not to tell it all at once. For example, when it comes to resolving a conflict or other dramatic interlude, or when following up a turning point, hints can be dropped or a future event or development mentioned and then you can leave your readers in suspense. They will want to read on to find out what happened next. By holding off the denouement until later in your work your readers will have to keep turning the pages.

Leaving your readers wanting more, especially at the end of one chapter, is normally described in fiction as a "cliff hanger." Although most autobiographies are not nearly so dramatic, if there was a conflict in your life and you had to make a decision or go off in a different direction - think about ending one section at that point. It is far more exciting to read than if you tell the entire story in one go.

Conclusion

This chapter has introduced a number of different techniques to help improve your writing so that it is more enjoyable to read. Although the actual story of your life may be fascinating to you, it is surprising how many autobiographies are never read as they are simply not interesting enough to people who were not there (rather like telling people your dreams or describing your holidays)! If you can introduce more of the senses, make sure readers are clear about what is going on, introduce some conflict and perhaps the odd metaphor or simile, your autobiography will be far more readable and enjoyable.

And now try this...........

Find a short scene you have already completed and write it again. This time, make it longer by improving it in some of the following ways:

- Use more of the five senses
- Introduce a metaphor or simile
- Can you add any point of conflict or suspense?
- Is it quite clear who is involved, what is happening, where and when it occurred, why decisions were made and how it all came about?

* * * * * * * * * * *

Chapter 6 - Show not Tell

Introduction

In the last chapter, we looked at ways to bring some life and colour to your writing. This chapter develops that theme in a particular way as it is all about taking your readers more into the story and encouraging them to become fully engaged with what is going on. As you know, if you are involved in a story it is far less likely that you will become bored and switch off and so it is very important for writers to bring immediacy to their writing in this way.

There are four different devices for achieving such an aim covered in this chapter:

- Show not tell – understanding what it is and how it is used
- Dialogue
- Small details
- Sentence structure

What does 'show not tell' mean?

If you find a piece of writing where someone's emotions are described in terms of how they behaved – for example, that they did something *angrily, happily, with a scowl* or they seemed *tired, bored* or *deliriously happy* the writer is TELLING readers how to view the people in this particular part of the story.

74

What you want to do is write in such a way that you clearly get across the emotions you are writing about without saying so in so many words, as it will be obvious that they are actually being experienced by your characters. So you need to recreate scenes in which readers can visualise people's feelings and emotions. By SHOWING readers what is going on they can make up their own minds about what they are seeing without you interpreting for them.

For example:

TELLING: *David was very angry with mother.*

SHOWING: *David looked at mother for a second. Then he ran across to the piano, picked up her favourite pottery vase and dropped it with a crash onto the piano keys, spilling water and flowers everywhere.*

Or here is another example:

TELLING: *Pauline was trying too hard to be attractive. She was heavily made up and smelled of too much perfume.*

SHOWING: *Pauline leaned towards her reflection as she finished drawing a thick line of bright red lipstick around her mouth. She checked her teeth with a grimace and then started sorting through the bottles of perfume that littered the surface of her dressing table. Geranium – no, too flowery. Musk – a bit obvious. Ah – her hand hovered over the little blue glass bottle she'd brought back from New York. That was perfect. She tipped the bottle into her hand and began dabbing perfume generously onto each wrist, behind her ears and into the hollow at the base of her throat.*

Activity 1

1. Find a descriptive piece you have already written that involves one or more characters and where their emotions

   Are described. If you do not have one write a few paragraphs about a memory that involves such a situation.

2. Now rewrite it *showing* the emotions rather than telling

   Readers what your characters were feeling.

Note that not all your scenes must be show and not tell – some telling is still perfectly acceptable. The aim should be to show as much as you can where it is appropriate. In this way, readers don't end up absorbing your writing passively but are actively engaged with it.

Dialogue

When it comes to showing emotions and feelings rather than telling, dialogue can be one of the very best methods possible.

Dialogue plays a vital role in bringing a scene to life, as well as being valuable in other ways that I will explain later. If you learn how to represent speech faithfully in the way it is *most likely* to have been spoken, so that it conveys a clear and true-to-life picture of the characters and personalities of the people having the conversation, together with their thoughts and feelings, you will find it adds enormously to those sections of your work where it is introduced.

By including the sort of phrasing, vocabulary and content in your dialogue that they would have used, they will be 'present' far more clearly – characters speaking their own words convey so much more about their background, education, emotions or the time in which they lived than you often can with straightforward description.

Writing dialogue is not easy and it does take quite a bit of practice. It is a question of tuning in to what people are saying and how they speak and slowly developing the skill of imagining and recreating realistic conversations. Although you may find writing dialogue hard, it is well worth while as it can bring your writing to life and make readers feel more involved.

There are also further good reasons to try to include some dialogue in your autobiography:

- It can move the story on
- It is an alternative way to provide information
- It can show conflict or add suspense
- It can set a mood – for example by introducing humour
- It can be a good way to show a turning point

*

> **Activity 2**
>
> Start listening to people talking on the bus, in cafes or the shopping queue, concentrating on phrases, vocabulary, the expressions they use, their rhythm and speech patterns and if they speak in whole sentences or just fragments. Make notes in your notebook to help you build up examples of phrases you could introduce into your writing.

Having suggested you include dialogue in your work, it is worth noting that you can also have too much. Unless you want to turn your autobiography into a play, you do need to use it sparingly. Aim for variety and contrast in any written piece by combining the two main styles of writing – narrative and dialogue – to keep readers engaged and wanting to continue.

Accuracy

At this point, I should acknowledge that some would-be autobiographers are concerned about the introduction of dialogue when the exact words cannot be accurate and may never have actually been spoken.

In my opinion, there is absolutely nothing wrong with using your imagination to summon up the spirit of people from your past using speech as a device. Unless writers have phenomenal skills of recall, the "dialogue" you read in most autobiographies or other non-fiction works cannot possibly have been remembered verbatim, or accurately represent a conversation word for word. Yet no-one reading the book would dream of calling the author a "liar" or start questioning their integrity.

Conventions when setting out dialogue

When including dialogue in a piece of work, the normal conventions are as follows:

- Surround all spoken words with "quote marks" and only add final quote marks when the same person finishes speaking, even if their speech extends over more than one paragraph.

- Place a comma at the end of a piece of dialogue, before the end quote marks and details of who is speaking

    E.g. "You were quite right," Irma said getting up.

- Place a comma in this way and also before the start of new quote marks if your speaker's details are positioned between two passages. For example:

"I was always told," John smiled meanly at Jessie as he spoke, "that little girls should be seen and not heard."

- Start a new paragraph every time a different person speaks
- Make absolutely clear who is talking. Sometimes you won't need any more than the words themselves, but if several people are joining in a discussion you don't want your reader confused about who said what to whom. One simple way is occasionally to include someone's name so that readers will know who is being spoken to. For example:

"Sheila, darling, I really think that is a silly idea."

- Now and again, change the position for details of who is speaking. As well as in the middle between parts of sentences, you can place these details at either the beginning or end of a spoken passage e.g.

  Jim spoke quietly: "Don't force me to do this."
  "Don't be daft, it will be fine," answered Harry.

- Although you may want to try a range of different words, using *said* is perfectly acceptable on a regular basis. Otherwise you can fall into the trap of looking as if you are trying too hard. The constant and relentless use of *cried, shouted, whispered, screamed* etc can become irritating.
- Take care not to use dialogue as a simple replacement for description. Try to use it for a purpose e.g. to show conflict – lots of short, snappy exchanges can be very effective – or to introduce change e.g. two people start agreeing but end up disagreeing, they start at loggerheads but end up with a sort of 'truce' or someone physically goes out of the scene.

Activity 3

1. Take an actual phrase or sentence you have written down in your notebook or that you hear on the radio or TV and try to develop it into a short imaginary piece of dialogue.
2. Think of an event from your past that involved you and one other person and write this up as a short conversation.

Improving your dialogue

Once you start to get the hang of dialogue, you may need to check that it is adding rather than detracting from your writing. Here are a few tips to bear in mind:

1. Less is more. Try not to include too many ideas when someone speaks, and cut out too much detail that will weigh the passage down. You are not writing real dialogue but "written" dialogue and so it must be focused, relevant and there for a purpose. Just replacing narrative with dialogue is not a good enough reason to include it

   For example: an exchange between two people about where to go on their holidays may be realistic but will not add to your story. If the dialogue reveals something about their characters, their relationship, if it builds the tension or if it shows that one of them has a hidden agenda, then it will be a valuable addition.

2. Don't spell it all out. If something is going on, a little intrigue can keep your readers guessing and so it can be a good idea to hold information back. In the same way, if you have previously introduced the subject of the conversation - such as an imminent house move or operation - you don't have to repeat the details all over again in your dialogue.

3. Remember to show not tell. Try not to end any dialogue with an adverb describing their emotional state (*he said sadly, angrily* etc) but show it in the words and description of the speaker.

4. Vary the scene structure. Stories that involve a combination of speech, action and description work much better than a large chunk of dialogue on its own as it helps maintain the pace of your material and keep your readers' interest. For example, when Jerry has previously told everyone how much he likes animals:

Jerry bent down and stroked Amber. Somehow he managed to catch her ear in his signet ring and she yowled and tried to bite him.

"My God, you little devil," he said, and without another thought gave the cat a swift back hander.

There was a brief silence and then we all watched as Margaret turned and walked quietly out of the room.

Activity 4

1. Find a piece of writing that you have completed and that at present includes a description of a conversation or other form of verbal communication.
2. Rewrite it to include some dialogue.
3. Compare the two to see if you feel the dialogue has added anything. In particular, check that it has moved your story on and is not just an alternative to using narrative.

Body language

As well as the words someone uses, their tone of voice and any dialect, communication also takes place non-verbally and so an equally important aspect is how they say it or what else is going on at the same time. Silences are very powerful and body language also tells you a great deal. You may therefore like to try to include some description of how people are behaving during any conversations. For example, to get over the fact that someone in your story is bored you could mention that they keep fiddling with their watch or are looking round the room as they speak.

Activity 5

Next time you overhear a conversation, note down what each person is doing with their hands, body, head etc as well as the words they speak.

<u>Small details</u>
Perhaps the most important piece of advice I can give you as an autobiographer is this: it is the small details that will bring your story to life.

Boring and bland passages, if you come across any in the books you read, usually have little or no variety or 'hook' to catch your interest, and they tend to be full of generalisations. They leave you feeling uninvolved and uninterested and may make you close the book altogether.

*

Activity 6

Next time you pick up a novel, look for the little factual details in the story. See how fiction writers use descriptions of clothes, household objects, mechanical workings or architectural features to help you visualise the place or objects as you read it including long detailed descriptions, being specific and mentioning immediately recognisable objects will often add a sparkle to your writing, as well as help readers visualise the scene and bring it to life. Quirky little facts are a particularly valuable device.

So, instead of describing someone driving a car, you can use the make and even model to help build character and enable readers to picture the scene.

If a piece of writing involved:

- a large, silver Chevy, or
- a small, cherry-red mini, or
- an old-fashioned London taxi

most readers would instantly be able to see the vehicle in their minds. So such details can only add to your story – particularly if there is a contrast between a character and the car they choose to drive! Details can also save a great deal of text, for example by instantly placing your characters in America or London.

Activity 7

Find a passage you have already written, or write up a new memory and make sure you add in some small extra details.

Sentence length

If you never vary your sentence length, your writing is likely to be monotonous to read. A passage full of long sentences is clearly likely to be a bit dreary, but lots of short sentences can also be unattractive as they make the piece choppy and unsatisfying. On average, short sentences are best when you want to convey a sense of action or faster pace or to get to the point. A long sentence allows you to develop an idea or describe something in more depth and can be more lyrical.

Activity 8

Take a reasonably long passage you have written and count the number of words in each sentence. Discover if you naturally write sentences that vary or if they are all a similar length.

Improving short sentences

If you tend to write too many short sentences, a quick 'fix' is to run several together with appropriate word changes or the use of conjunctions such as *but, although, whereas, after, and, then* etc.

We lived in Reading. The house was at the top of a steep hill. Mum had painted the walls a bright red
Becomes:
We lived in Reading at the top of a steep hill in a house Mum had painted a bright red.

Or
We lived in Reading. The house was at the top of a steep hill and Mum had painted the walls a bright red.

You also need to take care when joining sentences that the meaning is retained. For example, if you wrote the following:

Peter tore up the letter. I threw the ring at him.

Did you mean:
Because Peter tore up the letter I threw the ring at him.

Or:
Peter tore up the letter *but I still* threw the ring at him.

Or
Peter tore up the letter *and at the same time* I threw the ring at him.

Rewriting long sentences

To shorten some of your sentences, there are several different methods you could try.

- Break them into several shorter sentences
- If they become too short for you, join them using semi-colons. This is an acceptable way to combine two separate sentences that either have a main idea in common or two contrasting ideas. For example: *It was too hot. I could hardly walk and felt dizzy*

Becomes:

It was too hot; I could hardly walk and felt dizzy.
- Change from the passive to the active voice. For example: *The hedge was being trimmed by Uncle Jack*

Becomes:

Uncle Jack trimmed the hedge.

- Remove unwanted repetition (such as people's names) and wordy phrases e.g. "*In my own mind I began to wonder if ...*"

Becomes:

"I wondered if ....."

Activity 9

   1. Describe an event from your past in a way that contains lots of short sentences.

   2. Write it again but this time in the form of a few long sentences.

   3. Decide if your work is improved by either method and if you need to work on this aspect of your writing.

Conclusion

You will now have looked at your own style of writing and will have some ideas for making changes where you believe you could add immediacy and variety. In this way, you will hopefully ensure that your readers stay glued to the page rather than being turned off by any part of it.

And now try this.....

Some of the areas covered in this chapter are quite hard to introduce into writing if you are fairly new to them, although perhaps adding extra details and varying sentence length are less so. Write a short piece that includes examples of both 'show and tell' and some dialogue and also any other aspects covered so far in the book that you may be having trouble with. If you are rewriting material you are not happy with, ask a friend to compare them and see how much improvement the changes have made.

****

Chapter 7 - Filling in the Gaps

Introduction
After using a variety of methods to get in touch with your past, you will probably still find some areas are vague or even completely blank. One more memory jogger is introduced in this chapter that should help you in your task if you find that, despite practising all the exercises and techniques, you are still struggling on your own.

There are also different ways to fill in any gaps which will help build up the picture you are trying to present. As you are writing stories and describing scenes that need to be enjoyable for readers, it is important that they are 'complete'.

By spending some time researching the relevant time periods and exploring the setting or context in which a particular section of your life is set, you may discover or be reminded of various extra facts, figures and small details that you can add that will definitely enhance your tale.

Talking to people
One important memory jogger not covered in the earlier chapters is a fairly obvious one – and that is to talk to people from your past about your shared experiences. They may have a different view of the same events or characters you knew, but they are very likely to be able to fill in some valuable gaps and help you explore that period in some detail. It can also be very enjoyable just to reminisce!

Activity 1

Make a list of all those people living today who you could talk to over the phone, communicate with by email or letter or actually meet in person.

If your list is quite short, try again but, first, look through other memory joggers you have used such as the time line, CV or list of roles you have played. Many other people may suddenly suggest themselves. Here is a brief example:

School days – brothers and sisters, distant cousin who went to the same school, several school friends you still keep in touch with, one teacher you know is still alive. Also – what about the child of a neighbour who goes to the school now, so you can compare it to your day and perhaps remind yourself of those times as you talk about the school as it is today?

Activity 2

Think of a way to get in touch with at least one person you haven't spoken to for some time who would enjoy talking about a shared period from your past.

Set the meeting as a goal to achieve before you reach the end of this book.

Tracing people

This can be tricky, especially those you have lost contact with some years ago, but the Internet contains numerous reunited or social networking sites that your old contacts may have joined and you can leave messages for them.

Interviewing

With some of the people you meet up with, it will probably be a social event, but you may decide to go and visit someone less familiar – like an ex-teacher, employer or the elderly friend of one of your parents – and here it could be more of an interview.

For you to get the most from the encounter, if interviewing is unfamiliar territory, you need to be aware of different styles of questioning.

There are two main types of question you can ask: Closed and Open.

A <u>Closed</u> question allows the person in theory to answer simply Yes or No, although they will normally expand on the topic. It means you are steering the conversation and, very often, not getting to the real answers because you will find it hard not to make assumptions and guess what they want to say and so lead them towards saying it. In these circumstances, people are usually too polite to disagree or go off in a different direction.

Closed questions usually start with words such as:
Did you........
Was it ....
Have you........
Is it true that ....
Couldn't they have ....

<u>Open</u> questions allow your interviewee to answer in any way they see fit, and this is far more likely to throw up the interesting details and views that will inform your autobiographical writing.

Open questions start with words such as:

Where were you when.......

What was it like when ....

How did they react...........

Why did you ....

When did all this.............

Who was involved ....

Here is a quick example of the different and fuller answers you can get with Open and Closed questions and how Closed questions set up the answer in advance:

Closed: <u>Was it very hot</u> when you lived in France? Yes, certainly it could get so hot we had to spend most of the afternoons inside.

Open: <u>What was the weather like</u> when you lived in France? Well, it was very hot for most of the summer, of course, but I do remember the terrible floods in 1953........................

Activity 3

Find someone to help you and practise asking a series of Closed and then Open questions about any topic e.g. their last holiday, their work or a leisure activity.

See in which direction the different styles of questioning lead.

Telling the truth

Your autobiography is only YOUR view of your life and so other people who were there at the time may well have a different memory of a particular event or relationship. Although you will certainly want to bear that in mind and may, on reflection, decide to leave some details out, it is important that you don't end up writing someone else's view of your life as it won't feel right or 'true'.

You need to be prepared for the fact that, sometimes, the way you remember things may upset some people and hurt their feelings. What if you distinctly remember your sister being thrown out of the house but your father believes she left by choice and is angry at the suggestion? Or if you know your best friend had been very unpopular at school but she wasn't aware of this and would be hurt to discover it in your book? Or if you had been told that a family heirloom, an engagement ring, that your great aunt gave to her son for his new wife had actually been sold straight away?

There are several ways to deal with these sensitive issues:
1. Show or send the relevant passages you have written (even just in draft form) to anyone mentioned in your book, or to one of their close relatives or friends who may be upset by it, and consider their reaction carefully before deciding whether to cut, change or go ahead and leave it as it is.
2. Remove any material that could possibly upset anyone.
3. Leave all the details as they stand, once you have decided they are important for your story, and be ready to defend yourself against any criticism.
4. Before writing the final version, try to discuss the topic with the person involved. You may come to some agreement on the 'truth' that is acceptable to you both.

Activity 4

Thinking of one person you would like to talk to about your shared past – whether or not it would touch on any sensitive issues - note down 5 or 6 Open questions you might ask that would help fill in some gaps.

Research

As your story is all in your head, there is no requirement for you to do any research at all into facts, figures or other matters. However, you may find that spending a little time on these things contributes greatly to your writing and is definitely worthwhile.

Here are five different reasons to carry out some research rather than relying exclusively on memory:

1. It adds interest for people who like to know a little more about the time or place you are covering in your story. It can add texture and heighten the atmosphere or answer questions your material may raise.
2. You get the facts straight
3. It stops you being vague
4. It fills in gaps
5. You can add authenticity e.g. by including actual quotes from reference material

Getting the facts straight

Facts tell us much more than you may think. For example, if you know that someone is writing about the 1940s rather than the

94

1960s, or if they mention that the Prime Minister was Margaret Thatcher rather than James Callaghan, you will immediately have quite a different view of the social setting in which they were living without them having to spell it out. It can therefore be extremely important to include some factual information in your story to help you set the scene.

Small details are also very important, but if you want to describe the braid on the uniform an army officer was wearing, or explain the significance of a particular programme that was shown on TV when you were little, you may need to carry out some research to make sure you have the facts right. Otherwise, someone who knows these things and reads inaccurate details or dates in your autobiography will be very irritated.

It can be worth taking quite a bit of trouble over this because, as I have already mentioned, small details do bring your writing to life compared to writing about everything in a generalised way.

Activity 5

Consider one particular episode in your life story, particularly if it is already written up. What factual information could you add to enhance this piece of work?

Write a few sentences or rewrite an appropriate section with these details added.

Where to find the facts

When it comes to known facts in the public domain, there are several places you can go to check out information ranging from people's names to the dates certain things took place, locations for special events, when pieces of equipment were invented or were available to buy or what laws were passed and their exact wording.

Activity 6

Make a quick list of all the places you could go to find such information.

The Internet

The most obvious place most of us start when searching for information nowadays is the World Wide Web.

Using the URL (website address)

If you know the name of an organisation holding the information, you can go straight to their website and search there.

For example, if you know that someone in your story was involved with the Royal Society, their website address is likely to be www.royalsociety.org as organisations and charities have a URL ending in **.org**. Once you reach the site, institutions and organisations usually have a link to pages about their history, past presidents, fellowships and other material that you can read through to find your facts.

If you want to include details of the opening of a university building that you attended, you can easily go to the website of the educational establishment as their URL will end with.....**ac.uk** and you can then search their archive pages for details of the function and who else attended.

If the information is not readily available, these websites will also have contact details and so you can write, phone or email with your query and they are likely to be happy to help you if they can.

Reference websites

Some websites are there just to give you information. These include dictionaries, encyclopaedias and sites that offer information on how things work. My favourite for autobiographers would be www.wikipedia.org which is a vast encyclopaedia written by members of the general public.

Use a Search Engine

For many of the facts you are seeking, there is no easy starting point and so you will need to use a search engine such as www.google.co.uk. Decide on the most appropriate set of words that sums up your query and then type your key words into the Query box on the page.

If you don't often search the Internet, here are a few tips on the best way to carry out a search:

- Put words inside "quote marks" to search for a complete phrase
- Use + or AND or – or NOT in front of words that must be included or excluded
- Use a wildcard * symbol to search for words where certain characters are unknown or to encourage the widest search. For example, *pin* will find web pages

containing the words *hatpin, Le Pin, Chip and Pin, unpin* and *spin.*

For example, if you needed to know the name of the Prime Minster who presided over the 3-day week and wanted to write about what was happening politically at that time, you could type in *Prime Minister "3-day week"*. A list of all relevant websites will be displayed and you can follow any of these up to search out your missing details.

In many cases, you will need to think like a detective, following up clues until you hit on the elusive information. For example, a general search for details about what was going on in a particular country when you were living there may turn up the names of associations or forums that would enable you to contact or even hold conversations with others who were living there at the same time. You might also find the research acts as another memory jogger as you might discover the name of a country club you had joined but forgotten until now, something about your riding school, mention of a hotel you frequented and many other useful institutions, places or people that could help you fill out sections of your book.

Activity 7

Think of a subject you would like to find out more about such as a place you once lived or employer or institution you once worked for. Carry out an Internet search on your chosen subject and note down any interesting facts you could incorporate into your writing.

Local resources

Before the Internet came into our lives, reference material was usually found in the library or by accessing public records such as parish registers, the electoral register or documents held at Somerset House.

Libraries

Visiting the library may suit you far better than working on your own with a computer, but bear in mind that using a reference library means you usually have to take notes on site as you cannot take the books home with you. Make sure you take a note of any reference numbers on documents so they can be revisited later, and if you are allowed, take a few photographs of relevant pages.

Libraries offer maps, prospectuses, yearbooks, historical documents, dictionaries, biographies, travel guides, old photographs, journals and magazines and historical records that are kept on microfilm or in bound volumes.

Some libraries also contain material relevant to their particular location. One example is *Imagine York* created to showcase photographs of York held by City of York libraries and the city archives. This will allow you to walk forgotten streets or view places that no longer exist.

Once you have joined a library, you can also access for free a vast amount of subscription–only electronic reference material such as Credo Reference (400+ published reference works), the Oxford Dictionary of National Biography, Ancestry's Library Edition (a genealogy database) or News UK, containing international, national and regional newspaper full-text articles.

The British Library website (www.bl.uk) allows you to access thousands of records by searching by time period, subject, industry, region or language. You can find letters and documents of British sovereigns, their families and the royal household; early parliamentary diaries; archives of leading statesmen and prime ministers; and papers on numerous politicians, diplomats, colonial governors and other civil and military officeholders. It even holds data on a century of children's games and rhymes.

If you have a specific period or area of study, it is worth asking a qualified librarian to help you in your search as they will be able to recommend the most valuable resources.

Activity 8

Visit your local library and look closely at how the reference material is organised and what resources are available locally or in the area of particular relevance to past events in your life.

You could also ask the librarian to help you explore one particular section of your life story that you need more details about.

Public Records

Many local records are now online and there is usually a link via your library website. Examples include parish registers, the census, the general register office and valuation rolls. Some libraries also have other resources such as photographic archives or the military history of local regiments. The local records office may also have useful information and these now come under local government and can be accessed via county council websites (with the format www.(county Name.gov.uk) To actually view records, contact them or visit your county council offices.

There are many websites aimed at people tracing their roots that could help you research a particularly relevant part of your family history and these may be a good starting point. They offer links to the various public record websites and have information about wills, census returns, births, marriages and deaths. Some ask for a subscription, but just joining for a month or so may be all you need.

Two that might be worth trying are www.ancestry.co.uk as they offer a 14-day free trial, or the free www.british-genealogy.com

Historical and other associations
A different but valuable resource can be your local history society, local museum group, workers' clubs, car clubs, sports clubs, veterans groups, school associations or other specialist associations and societies. These are usually formed by enthusiasts who want to keep in touch or contribute to local knowledge by keeping the memories of past eras alive and who collect together important artefacts such as documents, recorded voices, relevant books or photographs that might otherwise be scattered or lost. If there is no active society you may still find bibliographies listing all the books that have been published about a particular area or employer.

*

Activity 9

For a place or establishment you would like to find out more about, see if you can locate a relevant society or association that either has a website or secretary you could contact.

Details

To add colour to your writing, you will remember that the little details need to be included. So 'a yellow flower' is more vivid to readers if you write about a sunflower or primrose; a 'fruit with seeds' is more recognisable as a papaya or pomegranate; and 'a car' speaks to readers if you tell them it was a mini or a Rolls Royce.

If you don't know the name of the flower, fruit or car, research is the only way to discover it and so be able to add it to your writing. Depending on the item, you will need to think creatively about where to go for the information.

For example, to discover the actual name of a flower, you could:

• Look in a plant book

• Visit a garden centre

• Talk to someone who knew the plant you mean

• Describe it on a gardening website forum

Corroborative evidence

When you want to describe something from your past in more detail than you can recall, the ideal is to go and walk round the place or examine the actual or an identical object. If you cannot do this with a place, building or item, you may find it valuable to seek out similar examples available today.

For example, an estate agent's details of houses in the area you once lived in that are of a similar design could provide valuable extra information to help you remember more about your childhood home. And the tour of a brewery would certainly help remind you of the technical terms or structure of at least some of the equipment you might once have used.

Museums are wonderful places to reawaken memories and add detail to your work. Static displays of interiors are often furnished with all the gadgets, textiles, furniture and clothing that were commonly available and used during a particular time period and if you are trying to relive the 50s, 60s or 70s, for example, you will probably go round identifying with the curtains, cushions or crockery that you remember from those times.

Working museums are also powerful reminders of how things were and if you want to relive the experience of life in a mill, the sound of steam engines, working in a chocolate factory or travelling on the top of a tram, you should be able to find a relevant museum to visit. You may find that churning butter, using tools or watching demonstrations or videos of milking and cheese-making or thatchers at work, together with listening to the sounds or recorded commentary will bring many more details back to you.

Period flavour

As well as exact dates, names, places or events, your writing will be further enhanced if you can flesh out the details with period flavour. Reading books and watching films covering a particular time can all be of great value in helping you relive some of your past. Working class life in the north of England, for example, is beautifully represented in books such as *Kes* and *The Loneliness of the Long Distance Runner* as well as the film *The Full Monty*. A good starting point for your explorations is "*The 20th Century Day by Day*" published by Dorling Kindersley. It details the key events in politics, war, religion, culture etc. for every year since 1900 and includes hundreds of photographs.

Activity 10

List some books or films that cover a period or a place that you want to write about and try to read or see some of them before finalising that particular section in your autobiography.

Conclusion

There is a vast amount of information out there that may help you add valuable details to the memories you have of your life. Some will require visiting places or reading books, documents and web pages or contacting people from the past but you will find that the effort is worthwhile as your writing will be more enjoyable and readable than otherwise.

And now try this....

Write a new section, or completely rewrite one you have previously written, so that it now incorporates some extra factual information. Either base it on a discussion or correspondence with someone from the past or from new research you have carried out.

* * * * * * * * * * *

Chapter 8 - Organising the Material

Introduction

Having got this far through the book, you will now have a large collection of memoirs, stories, anecdotes and other written pieces about your life. These need to be put together in a way that makes them enjoyable and understandable for your readers.

You will also have embarked on a personal journey that will have given you much to think about and perhaps helped clarify who you are and what life and your experiences mean to you. Knowing this can give you a consistent viewpoint from which to organise your account of your life.

Even if you are simply hoping to bring all the various contributions together in book form, rather than write an actual autobiography, you still need to think through the structure and make logical connections between the various items.

Knowing your audience

For any book or even quite short piece of writing, there is always a reader. As a writer, it is very important to have that person in mind as this will often determine the style and content of the material you produce.

Activity 1

List 5 people or groups of people who you think are likely to want to read your life story. Then decide which one you believe is the most important.

Here is a possible list:

- Yourself – particularly if you see it mainly as a therapeutic exercise in writing and remembering
- Your children – for them to treasure when you have gone
- Other close family members including your parents, spouse, siblings or grandchildren as a way to remind them of shared memories
- More distant relatives including in-laws, nephews and nieces or descendants not yet born, as an addition to their understanding of your family history
- Members of the general public who might be interested in particular areas of your life, for example as a part of our social history. These can be on any aspect such as early school days, life in the 1960s, bringing up children in rural England, living abroad or being a volunteer etc.

As this list covers a broad spectrum, it demonstrates that there are a number of issues to consider when you get down to the organisation of the material and, later, the final editing and rewriting of any passages.

Writing for children

If your primary audience will be grandchildren or other young readers, your childhood will be of particular interest as they will want to compare it to their own. Descriptions of how you responded to novelties such as colour TV, mobile phones, computers or holidays abroad – things they now take for granted - can also be a way to inject humour or show them familiar things in a new light. The tone you use will be very important; chatty and informal is likely to be the most appropriate for these readers.

Writing for close family

You will need to think carefully about the feelings of family members when they come to read your work – as discussed in Chapter 7. Also, it is natural to look for your own name when reading a relative's autobiography and wonder about their view of your relationship or to learn more about areas of life you don't actually remember very well yourself. Will you be including everyone and if not, will they be upset to be left out?

Making assumptions

Bear in mind that many names you mention or events that you allude to and may assume everyone knows about may not be familiar to readers in the future or those who are years younger than you. Jargon and the technical terms attached to many activities can also slip in which could be hard for general readers to understand. To avoid such confusions or the risk of losing your audience, always include a brief introduction or set things in context when mentioning anyone or anything for the first time.

Activity 2

1. If you are now clearer about your main audience, read through one passage you have previously written that you feel is at least in final draft form and check that the tone, content and style of writing are appropriate.

2. If not, rewrite it in a more appropriate style.

Finding a basic structure

The books that tend to remain in the mind long after they have been read are those with a theme or an idea behind them with which readers can identify. If you've been very lucky, you may have found a theme emerged as you were remembering and researching your past life. For example, your story may be one that fits into a recognisable category such as "rags to riches", "love conquers all", or "new beginnings". You may have spent your life overcoming adversity or you may have been searching for and found your roots. If this is the case, structuring your book should be much easier. If no such theme has emerged for you, organising your work will normally come down to a choice between two different methods:

- Chronological or date order
- Divided up into a number of different categories or headings

---

Activity 3

Think about how you want to structure your material. If a theme has emerged or you have an idea already, note down how it will work throughout the book.

If you don't yet have a basic idea, look through your material including your time line and decide which would be the better way to organise an autobiography – by date or under different categories.

Chronological order

It is quite likely that you will have gathered more material covering some periods of your life than others. You may have been given help by other people over certain parts or been able to remember some periods in greater detail. You may also have found photos, letters or diaries covering a particular time span that have helped you remember far more than you are able to for other sections.

This is not a good reason to structure your finished work in the same way!

To produce work that you are proud of, you should really make a positive decision about its scope. Here are two questions to consider:

- Is there one part of your life that you feel is more important than any other? This could form the bulk of your work with other material filling in lesser details.

- Would you prefer to complete several smaller books, each one covering a particular time period?

If the answer to both questions is No, you will need to make sure that the various chapters or sections of your autobiography balance out well enough for it to feel comfortable as readers work through it.

As a typical example of a well-balanced chronological autobiography, Eva Hoffman's 'Lost in Translation' has three sections covering her childhood in Poland (Paradise), life after emigrating to Canada (Exile) and later life in America (The New World).

Subset of time

Even when you want to write in chronological order rather than under various themes, there is no rule that says you have to include everything you ever did. You can choose whether to cover most of your life in some way or if you only want to concentrate on certain parts.

Some auto-biographers prefer to limit their books to a specific section of their life. This could be as short as one journey (for example Jenny Diski's *'Strangers on a Train'*), one year (as in Peter Mayle's *'A Year in Provence'*) or schooldays (as in Stephen Fry's *'Moab is my Washpot'.*) Even a span of 10 years is fine, as Alan Davies has shown in his recent book *'My Favourite People and Me'* covering the years 1978 – 88.

So, if you want to cover only the years from school to your first job, just your working life, the period between your marriage and the birth of your first grandchild or even just your retirement years, it is perfectly acceptable as long as you make a positive decision to do so.

Activity 4

Imagine you have decided to write your story in roughly chronological order. Note down 8 – 10 possible chapter headings that would cover the period of life you will be writing about.

Categories

If you prefer to write in a more unstructured way, covering your life outside the constraints of moving through time in one dimension, your categories may still be loosely chronological e.g. school days, university life, married life, living abroad etc but they could stretch unevenly across the years or be introduced in quite a different order.

You might prefer to base your chapters on broader themes with practically no years or dates attached such as *parenting* (for example as seen from the viewpoint of a parent, grandparent and foster parent), *spiritual matters, coping with disability* (yours and members of your family), or *marriage and divorce* (if you have had several or hold strong views).

Several books available today that have moved completely away from the idea of an autobiography in date order are:

- Joanna Lumley's *'No Room for Secrets'* where she sets each chapter in a different room in her house and readers are taken round as if guests, hearing the stories of the various objects and furnishings.
- Dawn French's *'Dear Fatty'* which is a series of letters to various friends and relatives covering snapshots of her life in no particular order.
- Alan Bennett's *'Writing Home'* is in the form of a collection of material with no obvious theme that brings together talks, diaries and occasional journalistic pieces written over a period of about 20 years.

*

Activity 5

If you were to write about your life in terms of different categories or particular themes, make a list of 8 – 10 chapter headings that would form the basis for your autobiography. .

Deciding on content

However you organise your material, you will need to decide on the most important aspects to include. Then you will need to spend time cutting out any details that detract from these and might make your work boring or even unreadable. The ideal contents are likely to be: significant events or highlights, major turning points and things you want to be remembered for.

Working out the exact content of the chapters is likely to be an ongoing activity. You may prefer to use separate sheets of paper for each chapter so that you can add new thoughts and ideas as they come to you. Eventually, you will have a list of the various scenes that relate to your chapter heading. For example, if I decided on a chapter heading of *Teaching*, my contents might include:

- Training to be a teacher. Turning point – realising I was not going to succeed with my chosen age range of 4 – 8 year olds
- Teaching English as a Foreign Language training – highlight, learning Japanese
- Entering the world of adult education, literacy and numeracy – turning point, using a computer to help

students with their English and running my own class for the first time.

- Conclusion – finding how much I enjoyed working with adults and starting a new career writing IT books.

Activity 6

Taking any topic that might be one of your chapter headings e.g. a time period or category, identify all the scenes that could be included. Now reduce these to the main events or highlights, major turning points and a possible conclusion.

<u>Finding your voice</u>
There is quite a lot of talk in creative writing circles about 'voice' which is hard for novice writers to understand and very difficult to manufacture at will. In essence, your writer's voice is what makes your writing distinctive and different from other people's. It will most likely emerge only as your writing develops and especially if you read as widely as possible and write as often as you can.

Factors that can help identify a particular writer include:
- Their choice of vocabulary

- The length of their sentences

- The themes they choose to write about

- How passionately they put their ideas across

Activity 7

To help you understand about voice, think about a favourite author. Given an anonymous piece of writing, how would you know if it was written by them, rather than someone else?

Narrative style

You may have assumed that 'past tense narrative' was the only style in which to write your autobiography. For example: *"I was born in Russia in 1882 in a small town named Evanach."*

But many successful books or autobiographical works have used quite a different approach.

Activity 8

Look through the fiction and non-fiction books on your shelves and list the different ways that stories can be told. Add your own ideas to the list.

Here are some examples:

- Letters
- Poems
- Diary or journal entries
- Songs
- As a novel
- Linked short stories
- Travelogue
- Sermons

- Commentary accompanying photographs
- Dialogue or script for a play or film
- A scrapbook with writing interspersed with memorabilia
- A cookbook with stories about where the recipes came from

Changing the form of the narrative can sometimes make quite a difference to the finished work and may suit you more than writing using the standard format.

Activity 9

1. Take any scene or story you have written as a straightforward narrative and, choosing any of the above styles or one of your own that you came up with, rewrite it in that format.
2. Reflect on the experience and the quality of the storytelling using the two different methods.

If you cannot decide between several different styles, there is no reason why you cannot produce a multi-format book that includes a range of writing styles such as letters, poems and stories - or even a multi-media work that includes photos, letters and recipes as well. (This is not the right place to go into details but video and film cannot be ignored as fantastic ways to tell a life story, and working in this format may be something you would enjoy looking into.)

Co – authors

In most cases, you will be writing your autobiography on your own. If you think your book would work better as a compilation or in several parts, each section completed by someone different such as a partner, sibling or child, it is probably better if one person acts as overall editor. For consistency, they will need to set the style and one for the work and then ask for contributions that will fit in with the agreed plan.

Beginning and ending

As we have said, there is no requirement to cover the whole of your life in your autobiography and it is unlikely that you would be able to go from your birth up to almost the last day of your life. So you will need to make some decisions about where to start, where to end and how to structure the whole story. (You may even like the idea of your writing as a "full circle" and ending at the same point that you began!)

As well as the entire work, you must also remember that every chapter also needs a beginning and an ending.

- For an ending to your life story, you may find it best to finish with a significant event such as your retirement, a move abroad, reaching a particular age or your 50th wedding anniversary.

- To encourage readers to stay with you, you could end some chapters with a cliffhanger or a hint of what's to come. For example, you could mention the name of someone who will later play an important part in your life, or put in something that makes readers ask "Why?" or "What happened then?" - making quite sure you answer the question later.

- Match the tone of your story with its introduction. A humorous piece would normally start in a light-hearted way.

Here are some examples of starting points other writers have used for their autobiographical work:

- Aged 21 in New York (Barack Obama in *Dreams from my Father*)
- Country childhood (Nelson Mandela in *A Long Walk to Freedom*)
- His own birth (Roger Moore, *My Word is My Bond*)
- The middle of a West Indian cricket tour (Darren Gough in *Dazzler*)

Activity 10

1. Thinking about your life story, what is the earliest time you will go back to?

2. Where is the best place to end?

Flashbacks

There is no rule about the *order* in which you write. Many books and films (with *Pulp Fiction* being an extreme example) dot about between the present, the past and the future, although it takes some skill to make it all hang together.

Describing events that happened in the past after moving back from the present is known as *flashbacks* and these can be a

117

useful device if, for example you really want to start your story at a particularly exciting or eventful time but still cover earlier years. When you are describing an event and want to move forward quickly to a later period that bears some relationship to this time or event, you can use a *flash forward.*

As we saw in Chapter 5, the main thing to bear in mind is the need to make it clear to your readers where and when particular events are taking place. You also need to create credible links between the various time periods.

For example, if you have been describing an early episode and want to flash forward, you can mention the actual date or use phrases such as *"Many years later, I was....."* or *"It wasn't until I went to ......"* and continue the story from there.

Activity 11

1. Decide where you want to start your autobiography. This may be at the earliest period you have decided to cover or with a particular event or turning point using flashbacks or flash forward to introduce earlier or later episodes.

2. Write a short piece about a recent event involving someone you have know for some time, and include a flashback to describe that person when they were younger.

Questions

One common way to introduce an autobiography is to start by answering the question "Why am I writing this?" For example, if you got the idea after being asked a question about your past by one of your grandchildren, or if the death of a parent whose story you feel was unfinished made you want to tell your own story, you may like to begin your work with such an explanation.

Titles

There is nothing wrong with calling your autobiography *My Story* or *The Autobiography of .....* but you may prefer to use a more original or personal title for your life story.

There are different approaches to titles and it will depend on the content and tone of your material. For example you could use the title to give readers a clear idea or at least a clue as to its contents and scope e.g. *'The Last Fighting Tommy'* by Harry Patch, *'Dying to be Thin'* (about anorexia) by Nikki Grahame or *'School Blues'* by Daniel Pennac (about life as a pupil and then a teacher).

You also need to think about chapter headings as you might want them short and descriptive, neutral (Chapter 1, 2 etc), catchy or clever.

Here is a list of various sources you might use to find titles:

- Quotations from the Bible or classical literature
- Poems, hymns, songs, nursery rhymes or carols
- The works of Shakespeare
- A nickname you are known by
- Catch phrases from TV or radio
- Well-known sayings or proverbs e.g. *The Devil Makes Work for Idle Hands, An Early Bird (catches the worm)*

- Family sayings that will be instantly recognisable (but if you want to be read by a wider audience you may need to add an explanation or at least sub-title)
- People's names (a device used by Alan Bennett, for example, whose chapter titles have included *Uncle Clarance, Russell Harty* and *Peter Cook.)*
- Names of recipes, flowers, places etc.

You can also use different writing styles to give you ideas for titles e.g.

- Alliteration (each word starting with the same letter e.g. *Helping Hamsters in Hanover)*
- Puns – a play on words, perhaps involving your family name or a familiar saying or song title (e.g. '*Tanks for the memory*' about the war years)
- Spoonerisms (transposing words or letters e.g. *Roaring with Pain* instead of *Pouring with Rain)*
- A single word e.g. *Help, Success* etc.

Activity 12

Try to decide on a main title and titles for your chapter headings or at least the approach you will take to find them

---

Conclusion

In this chapter we have looked at how you can organise your work so that it reflects your own style and the type of story you are telling. You will have a good idea of how you want to structure your material, what to include or leave out and what you can title each part.

And now try this.......

Two of the activities in this chapter asked you to create a list of chapter headings; one in date order and one based on your selected categories or themes.

1. Look at both these lists, take into account any other factors covered so far and set out a definitive chapter list for your autobiography.

2. Taking a different chapter heading from that used in Activity 6, itemise the various topics or major events you want to cover e.g. highlights, turning points, what you want your readers to take away or things you want to be remembered for and any conclusions you can draw looking back on that time.

3. Write a couple of paragraphs that will be included in this chapter such as the introduction or a story covering one particular event.

****

Chapter 9 - Editing and Finishing

Introduction

So far, this book has concentrated on developing the skills of remembering, writing and revising your material and you will be applying these skills to every aspect of your life that you eventually decide to include. You should also by now have a good idea of how you want to organise your finished life story. So now is the time to look at the piece as a whole

The idea of editing and checking your work in detail hasn't been introduced before because use of English should never get in the way of the writing and remembering process. Only once you have more than enough material to include can you get down to the final stages of bringing it all together and making sure it is written as clearly and accurately as possible.

At this point, you may be flagging a little and wondering how you can keep going to achieve your ultimate goal, so at the end of this chapter I have included a few ideas to help sustain your motivation.

The writing stages

Some people approach all tasks in a systematic and logical fashion whereas others prefer to take a less structured path. However, if you want to complete a large and complex piece of work such as an autobiography it can help to do it step by step. Here is one way to approach your task:

122

a. Write everything down, in note form if necessary, to make sure you catch each memory before it disappears. This is the way to produce enough material to work with.

b. Once you have decided on how you want to relate your story, re-order your pieces of writing so that they are all in the right places. This may mean:

    1. collecting together events taking place over the same time frame

    2. introducing incidents at different times so that you can link them using flashbacks

    3. splitting up some anecdotes to create end-of-chapter cliff hangers or more suspense

    4. grouping items together because they are related to the same theme

c. Check that your work balances by cutting out extraneous, repetitive or unwanted details or even dropping whole periods of your life if they add nothing or – worse - turn your autobiography into a long-winded and boring saga.

d. Look carefully at every piece of writing you want to include and revise it so that it is lively, enjoyable and engages your readers.

e. Write the beginning and end, if they require special handling.

f. Check the basic grammar, spelling and punctuation.

g. Depending on the way you are presenting your life story, you may need to ask for and edit other contributions or collect together items of memorabilia if they are to be included.

Activity 1

1. Read through the list and decide if the order is right for you. If not, write down your own step-by-step approach.
2. Identify where you are in your list.
3. Check that you have completed everything covered by earlier steps before moving on (if they are not things that need to work in parallel).

Duplication

Some people, points of view or types of event can crop up throughout your life. If you have chosen to base your autobiography around different themes rather than set it out chronologically, you will need to be careful that you don't repeat yourself. (An exception is where you make a positive decision that this is the best way to emphasise a particular aspect of your life such as not seeming to learn from mistakes or life being a series of repeated patterns.)

It should be fairly easy to avoid duplication once you've decided on the detailed contents of each chapter as there will either be a reason for including the same thing again or it will appear to fit most comfortably in one place.

If it still seems to be a problem, decide on the most appropriate place to mention the people involved or to describe the particular events and then cut out any reference to the same thing in other sections of your writing.

Additions and deletions

In the last chapter you identified your main audience. With them in mind, you may need to add extra material, for example if you have left out one person for no particular reason and you now realise they would definitely feel excluded. Having decided how you are going to approach true but upsetting facts, you will also need to make a final decision about whether to delete or leave in particular anecdotes or views.

More subtle, but still important may be the need to change the emphasis or tone. Now that you are considering your autobiography as a whole, it may also become clear if perhaps there is too much or too little mention of someone, something or some events and now is the time to redress the imbalance.

Activity 2

Repeat the exercise you carried out to list the contents of one chapter with all or at least several more chapters. Now check that there is no duplication, all gaps can be filled and there is no other material that you should leave out altogether or emphasise more or less than you originally intended.

Consistency

There is nothing more irritating in a book than finding that the style suddenly changes part way through, and so it is important to read across all your material (or at least finalised examples from a number of chapters) to make sure that you are writing in the same way about similar things.

Style includes the pace, vocabulary, sentence length (except where you are deliberately introducing change), viewpoint and the balance between description, action and dialogue. If you are not writing a standard narrative, even poems or plays still need to be consistent throughout.

It is unlikely to happen in an autobiography so much as fiction but you must also take care that you are not jumping around too much between facts that you are aware of and tales told by others. If your readers are following "your" point of view, it is disconcerting if you suddenly start describing something that you couldn't have experienced and that is actually someone else's view of the events. Again unlikely, but check that you haven't suddenly moved between present and past tense or from first person to third unless it is quite deliberate.

Activity 3

Read examples of several pieces of writing taken from different parts of your book and make sure they are all written in the same style.

Grammar, punctuation and spelling

Have you ever sent off a substantial piece of written work, a letter or even an email and realised, too late, that it contains various errors you could easily have put right? Anyone who has had that experience knows that it is extremely important to check your finalised work in some detail. If you are particularly weak on grammar or spelling, do get help from a friend or relative as it will be too late (or certainly very expensive) to correct any errors you spot once the book or other publication is in the public domain.

As I don't know what level of education you have reached, I will not patronise you with a proper English lesson. But even if you are someone who has excellent writing skills, it is surprising how many people trip up over some of the less common grammatical and other rules. So I will just cover a few specific aspects.

Grammar

Paragraphs

Once you have written a section of your autobiography, one decision that may need to be made is whether or not to break up the text into two or more separate paragraphs. If a piece of work has ever been criticised as being difficult to read, it may simply be because you have packed too many ideas together into a single block of text, making it long-winded and indigestible.

To improve any written work, check that each paragraph is really about a single topic or field of interest and, if in doubt, start a new paragraph at a point of change. You should also think of starting new paragraphs simply to cut down on the amount of text in a single block.

Formal or informal English

Documents that will be read by anyone except very close family or friends are normally written using more formal English, unless you have deliberately chosen an informal 'voice', This means you may need to take care that you are not using slang or too many casual phrases that might be out of place.

Apart from in a piece of dialogue, it is often the case that written words chosen to be *read* are slightly stiffer than spoken words, and obviously you would never write verbatim as you would not want to include ums, errs etc in a piece of narrative! So, as an example, it *may* read better to use the phrase "it was not possible for me . . .." rather than "I just couldn't...."

If in doubt, try out formal and informal versions and decide on the most appropriate for that particular section of your autobiography.

Activity 4

Find any long passages in your writing and make sure you are happy with paragraph length and the formal or informal style you have chosen.

Punctuation

There are three punctuation symbols that are constantly used incorrectly in newspapers and magazines, on notice boards and shop fronts and in other public places. These are the apostrophe, the colon and the semi-colon.

<u>Apostrophe'</u>

There are only two places where the apostrophe is required:

- to show possession
- to replace missing letters

It is NOT used in plurals such as "The shop was selling cheap **bananas**."

Possession: here you must concentrate solely on the *owner* of any object or objects, no matter how many objects they own. You place the apostrophe immediately after the identity or name of the owner/owners and, if required, add an **s.** If the word ends in s, you normally do not add another one. Even if the owner comes at the end of a sentence, the rule still applies.

If one boy owns a banana, it is the **boy's** banana
Or: The banana is that **boy's**.
If a boy owns several bananas, they are the **boy's** bananas
If two sisters share one cat, it is the **sisters'** cat
If two sisters have a cupboard full of shoes, they are the **sisters'** shoes.

Possessive pronouns do not add apostrophes e.g. **his, its, theirs** and **yours** stay as they are.

When using plural nouns, place the apostrophe straight after the plural: a **child's** toys or several **children's toys**, a single **man's** fence or several **men's** fence

Missing letters (contraction): You will be familiar with the words *can't, won't, hasn't, shan't, doesn't* – these are all contractions of *cannot, will not, has not, shall not* and *does not*
More awkward are contractions of *they are, he is* and *it is* – these become *they're, he's* and *it's*.

For example:

Referring to a tortoise: *Its* shell looks heavy....... (Possessive pronoun)

But you could also say about the shell: I think *it's* heavy (Missing letters)

Colon:

The colon is used to introduce lists of things, statements or quotations.

For example:

- LIST – *I bought several things: a bag of sugar, a cabbage, three oranges and a newspaper.*
- STATEMENT – *One thing was clear: he had to leave.*
- QUOTATION - *Sally said crossly: "I've had enough."*

Semi-colon;

I have already mentioned in an earlier chapter how you can use a semi-colon to join two short sentences together. These can either be related to the same topic or are contrasting statements.

For example:

Peter was hungry; he set out for the pie shop.

The first week was boiling hot; the second week was cold and overcast.

You can also use a semi-colon in a complex list if the items would become confusing when separated only by commas.

For example: you would use commas to separate a shopping list of bananas, crisps, fish and milk.

If the items included *a very small, black dress that was meant to be drip-dry; a huge bunch of flowers wrapped in paper; a box of shiny, writeable disks; and a coffee,* the descriptions already contain commas and so each complete item needs to be separated more clearly from the next using semi-colons.

You can also use a final semi-colon in front of the last item even though it is introduced with a conjunction such as *and, but, or* etc.

Activity 5

If punctuation is your weak spot, go through your writing and check you are using these symbols appropriately.

Spelling

When you spell a word wrongly and you are not using the spell checker on a computer it is not much use telling you to check it as you will presumably have written it that way because that is how you thought it was spelt.

There are a few things you could do if you find spelling hard and have a history of getting errors picked up in any written work:

1. Ask a friend or relative to check your spelling
2. Always look up any word you feel unsure about in a dictionary or on an Internet dictionary website
3. Copy out a passage on a computer using a word processing package such as *Microsoft Word* to see which words are identified by the spell checker.

Proofreading for sense

You may have perfected your grammar, punctuation and spelling but when you read your own work, it is very easy to see words you didn't write or to miss silly little mistakes - or even major ones - that make nonsense of what you have written. These errors can only be picked up by reading everything through very carefully. It is also best to come to it cold, so wait some hours or a day before reading back work you have written. Errors can include:

- using words that are not actually spelt wrong but change the meaning e.g. I ate a **role** and butter
- duplicated words e.g. he was neither tall nor **nor** short
- transposition (changing letters round) e.g. he fought in the last **raw**
- using the wrong tense e.g. He *had* a nasty cold that **makes** him miserable and grumpy

More importantly, you need to read through each chapter to make sure you haven't written a whole sentence twice, cut and pasted the wrong material or – common when copying out from hand written notes – introduced the wrong section of text in the wrong place.

As well as checking work on a computer screen, it is a good idea to print out material as it can be easier to spot mistakes on the printed page. If you can, ask someone else to go through it as well as they may see things you've missed.

Activity 6

Take one section, read through very carefully and see if you pick up any mistakes you previously overlooked.

Using a computer

Right at the start I said you don't have to use a computer for writing an autobiography. However, it certainly makes life very much easier. You can:

- Keep copies safe by saving your material onto removable media such as flash drives or CDs
- Always have written work that is easy to read and can be printed and sent to people or emailed out
- Make it straightforward to cut and paste and move chunks of your book to different positions
- Add new material into a section already completed
- Use the spelling and grammar checking facilities (although never rely on these completely)

There are also lots of techniques possible in word processing applications such as the option to create an outline for the whole book, add a table of contents or index, review changes you have made or add page numbers, headers and footers (e.g. to display the chapter title and your name on each page) and the current date. If you are unfamiliar with a computer, it might be worthwhile having a few lessons or buying a simple "How To..." book and use this opportunity to improve your word processing skills.

Keeping on track

This chapter has been about looking at your material as a whole and making those last but vitally important checks that it is as you want it. However, you may be nowhere near finishing either a section or the complete works and you may be feeling daunted by the hill you still have to climb. When a writer (or anyone) faces this sort of challenge, you need to pump up the motivation and feel confident once more that you will get this job done. So here are two techniques taken from the world of life coaching that may help you.

SMART goal setting

A large task often appears so huge, we cannot face it and so use avoidance tactics. On the other hand, we can usually manage a single step forward. SMART goal setting involves identifying and then taking a series of small steps, one at a time, until you realise you have reached your ultimate goal.

For each step:

S stands for <u>specific</u>. This means you must set a very specific target. Instead of the vague idea of "talking to everyone who knew me at school", a specific goal would be to **phone up Susan Smith and arrange to have a chat about schooldays.**

M stands for <u>measurable.</u> Here you must set a target that can be measured e.g. in time, distance, number of pages written, boxes sorted or some other factor. So instead of phoning Susan to arrange to meet in a general sense, you goal could be to arrange to talk to Susan **when she is free for an hour.**

A stands for <u>achievable.</u> If Susan lives abroad or many miles away, arranging a meeting will be impossible by next week. So here your goal should be to **arrange a time we can talk over the phone for an hour**.

R stands for <u>realistic.</u> It won't work if you are overambitious and try the impossible. So if you have no idea where Susan Smith lives or what her phone number might be, you need to find someone else like Pam to talk to whilst trying to get hold of Susan's contact details.

T stands for <u>time sensitive.</u> Here you need to set a date or time by which you will achieve your goal. In our example, you could decide that you will have had the chat with Susan or Pam **by the end of next week**.

Whether you have achieved this first SMART goal or missed your deadline, you need to review progress. There are now two possible actions:

- Rewrite the goal (if it was still too ambitious or other circumstances got in the way)

Or

- Move on to the next step and set a new SMART goal e.g. based on the discussion **to write two pages about my schooldays by Thursday.**

Activity 7

Finish the sentence: *My SMART goal is to* .... and then set about achieving it.

Affirmations

This technique is not for everyone but there is some truth in the idea that, if you say something enough times you start to believe it and it becomes self-fulfilling. So if you tell yourself (*affirm*) that you will complete your autobiography, there is even more chance that this will turn out to be true.

For an affirmation to work properly, as you may be attempting the difficult task of changing your beliefs, it needs to be set up in the following way.

 a. <u>Decide</u> on the topic. In our case it will be related to completing your autobiography but it could be general e.g. become more self-confident or to enjoy life more.

 b. <u>Imagine</u> what it will be like if you are successful. Create a picture in your mind of how you will feel when your life story has been written and published. See people responding to a copy, and imagine the book on the shelf.

 c. <u>Write</u> your affirmation in the following format:

  a. In the first person

  b. In the present

  c. The wording must make you feel excited.

For example: *I am a great writer and people love reading my life story*

 d. <u>Repeat</u> your affirmation many times a day and, as you do so, run through the images you created in your mind when you imagined succeeding.

 e. <u>Say it out loud</u> and, if you feel like it, share it with other people.

 f. <u>Remind</u> yourself of the affirmation. Try writing it on small pieces of paper, or use pictures that summon it up, and leave these around where you will keep seeing them.

Activity 8

Write out an appropriate affirmation and have a go at repeating it, especially just before you go to sleep.

Overcoming writer's block

There may be times when the whole task you've set yourself or at least one part of it seems too much, and you find yourself sitting looking at a blank piece of paper without any idea of what to put down. This is a well-known phenomenon known as *writer's block*. If you worry it may happen to you or you have experienced it in the past, here are a few possible remedies:

- Establish a routine and stick to it. It is often easier to write when you *have to* rather than wait until you feel like it.
- Set realistic targets. Don't expect to write five pages a day, but set as a target something sensible and achievable like two paragraphs. When you've written that you may well feel like writing some more.
- Leave off in mid-flow rather than finishing a section or scene neatly, so that you won't have to start all over again next time. When you sit down to finish off the piece you left, you may find you get into a writing rhythm and have the energy to carry on to the next section.
- Impose a deadline. If you tell yourself you must finish a particular section or cover a certain time period by the end of the day, it may motivate you to keep writing.
- Start a diary or just write *anything* for five minutes. With no pressure to write well, just noting down

what you did yesterday or making a shopping list may get you back into writing mode.

- Do something constructive that is not writing. If you really cannot face the page, read someone else's autobiography, sort through some memorabilia or fill in an extra bit of your time line. Taking your mind off the task for a while may be just what you need.

Conclusion

Your autobiography, if your aim is to write a book, will now be well on the way to completion and you have all the tools to make sure it is well written and comes together as a whole. The final chapter introduces different ideas for telling your life story that not only include book publishing but also how to use aspects taken from the past to reach different audiences.

And now try this.......

Now is the time to work on a large chunk of writing – up to 4 pages or around 1,000 words – until you are happy it is completely finished. Having used all the advice in this book to make sure it is written clearly and engagingly, with your preferred emphasis and using the style of writing you are comfortable with, it should also be accurate in terms of editing and proof reading.

* * * * * * * * * *

Chapter 10 - Reaching a Wider Audience

Introduction

Hopefully you will have a large body of material including notes, stories, anecdotes, character sketches, vignettes and other writing based around your life. One aim of this book has been to help you gather this up and present it in the form of a complete autobiography. But if you also want to use it in other ways, or a book was never your goal, this chapter will show you different ways to tell your story (or stories) to others.

Readers' letters

Have you ever seen your name in print? For many people, having a letter published in a newspaper or magazine can be their first taste of fame and it can be quite intoxicating! With some publications, it can even earn you a little money – you may receive £5 or £10 and star letters offer prizes that can be worth £40 or £50 – but that should not be the main goal as usually you will receive nothing at all. When it comes to writing based around your past, there are certain types of letter that have a better chance of being selected for publication:

- Tips, hints or general advice e.g. old recipes, ways to save money, home remedies, solving gardening problems etc
- Reminiscence, particularly if accompanied by photographs e.g. showing the clothes you wore or places you knew
- A humorous or embarrassing incident

- Links with well-known celebrities you once met or worked with
- Comparisons between how things are done now and what went on in the past, particularly if you select a topical subject
- How to do something you were an expert in

The best magazines to try with these types of letter (or even just photographs with a few lines of explanation) are those aimed at older readers such as *Saga* or the fortnightly *Yours*, but you could also try general women's magazines. (Men often write these letters so don't be put off if you are not a woman!) Other publications may be more appropriate if the content of your letter relates to a specialist subject such as crafts, a regional slant, farming, waterways, TV programmes, parenting, boats, shopping (supermarket magazines are now common), dieting, model-making, horses, music or vintage clothes.

You will need to look through your target magazines (in shops or online if you don't subscribe or buy copies) to find out the address or email to write to. Local newspapers will usually be interested in stories from the past about the area or any change you can tell them about to buildings or amenities, especially if you have suitable photographs.

Activity 1

1. Think of a subject you could write a letter about that would fit one of the six categories listed above. Next time you go shopping, have a look at the magazine racks and see if you can find one covering your subject.

To make sure your letter is selected and not rejected:

- Read through some of the letters that have been published in your target publication to check on style and tone and set out yours in a similar way. For example, humour may feature strongly or they may prefer straightforward advice with bullet points.

- Always keep the length of your letter *shorter* than the longest letter published so they don't need to waste time editing it for publication.

- Try to make your point clear e.g. reminiscence has to be seen to have relevance. It could help provide an example of 'best practice,' include funny things you or other people said, offer advice based on a particular experience or may be better aimed at a regular page of readers' contributions such as "Weddings from the Past" or "Our Teenage Years"

Activity 2

Write a letter for a magazine. If you like the result, why not send it off?

Here is a tip I wrote that was published in *Somerfield* magazine:
"*Most people buy exotic fruit to eat – but then throw away the stones. For the past few years I have been putting these inedible parts to good use. I simply push any stones into small pots of*

ordinary garden compost and store them in the airing cupboard for about a month. Usually I find small shoots starting to show. I now have an amazing array of plants that includes lychees, star fruit, tangerines, lemons and mangoes."

Magazine articles

If you prefer to write a more substantial piece and want to be paid for your work, the next market you could try breaking into is that of magazine articles.

Many glossy magazines have their own staff writers and rarely look at amateur contributions. On the other hand, specialist and less glamorous publications rely heavily on input from new writers and it is a satisfying way to use the material you have spent time researching and reliving.

Other publications you could consider apart from magazines include specialist journals, newspapers or in-house newsletters and bulletins. For example, current employees may enjoy reading your experiences of the company in a 'looking back' piece.

Topics

Many of the approaches relevant to readers' letters can be applied here, but you will need to have enough material for a longer piece.

Here are some examples of possible types of article that could be published:

- Humorous incidents turned into a good story

- 'How to' articles such as "bringing up twins" or "running a youth football team"
- Photographs that tell a story
- Experience used to contrast how things were done then and now (e.g. *Christmas as an evacuee*)
- True stories or disasters with a dramatic content
- Confessions
- Technical know-how
- Tips and hints expanded into an article
- Celebrity nostalgia
- Reviews of books or films related to your past experiences

Activity 3

1. Think about the range of magazines you have already researched, as well as the other sources mentioned.

2. Looking back over your life, select a few topics or events that could be expanded into an article of around 750 – 1,000 words for a target publication.

Planning an article

If you write an article that needs to be published at a particular time of year, make sure you submit it at least six months in advance. Publishers plan their publications months ahead and you will miss the boat if your Easter story is sent in February.

Nowadays, with digital cameras so widespread, most editors expect their contributors to be able to provide photographs as

143

well as text. If you want to write about a particular subject that lends itself well to pictures, spend a few weeks taking suitable shots. Set your camera at the highest resolution possible (so the pictures will print well) and store them on your computer. If you are using old photographs, you may need advice on how to convert them for today's publications if you do not want to send off the originals.

If you read several articles in your target magazine, you will see how they are normally structured, but if in doubt the most common approach is:

- Start with a 'hook' to draw in readers. This could be an observation that raises a question you then set out to answer, or an experience that provides the reason for writing.
- Follow with the main body of your article set out in suitably readable chunks or paragraphs, using sub-headings if it helps improve clarity
- End with a conclusion that rounds the article up or suggests further action the reader can take.

For example, I once wrote an article about taking an Inland Waterways RYA Helmsman's Course which was published in *Canals & Rivers magazine* which had the following structure:

a. My observation that I wasn't very confident about taking the boat out alone and I knew many other people felt the same way.

b. The suggestion that a training course might be the answer

c. A description of what was involved, costs, where to find courses etc.

d. My conclusion that it was worthwhile and had given me the confidence I had been lacking.

Activity 5

Plan out your article in draft form.

The Query letter

Unlike readers' letters, there is often no point in writing an article in its entirety and sending it to a magazine on spec. Instead, you may need to get the agreement of the editor that they want your article and to sort out such things as word count, the exact approach, any extras e.g. side bar notes, tips and hints that can go in a box or suggested further reading, what sort of pictures may be required etc. before getting down to the writing.

The first contact you make is known as the *query letter*, and nowadays it is quite acceptable to send this in the form of an email. Carry out a little research online or by phone to discover the name and contact details of the overall editor or an appropriate features editor as it is important that you write to them in person. Otherwise, your query letter may disappear somewhere in the system. Here is the information they will need to receive:

1. What your article would be about
2. A suggested (working) title – although this is often changed before publication
3. Why it is appropriate for their publication (for example, it might form part of a series they are currently running)

4. Why you are the best person to write it (i.e. your relevant experience, details of any published work etc)
5. If you have suitable photographs to offer
6. Where there is likely to be a delay (perhaps because you need to make some visits or carry out research), when it would be ready for publication.
7. Questions you need to ask e.g. what length and format, how many pictures and any special features they would want you to include.
8. Your full contact details.

Activity 6

1. Write a query letter.
2. If you feel confident, send it off and be prepared to write the article for real!

Fiction

So many books and courses are now available on writing novels, poetry, plays, children's books, blockbusters, short stories or even song lyrics that I won't spend time giving advice about them here. Suffice it to say, many are autobiographical in nature – whether overtly, unintentionally or disguised – and you may already have come across past experiences that you would enjoy writing up in this way.

The only thing to bear in mind is that, as soon as you publish anything, family members, friends and colleagues will read your work looking for references to themselves. You may have some explaining to do even if the characters are not based on anyone you know.

Talks and broadcasts

When speaking about the past, you can either prepare a piece word for word or take part in a more informal way.

Face to face

For those of you who enjoy public speaking or working face to face, one enjoyable area to explore when considering how to find an audience for autobiographical material is that of giving talks or running workshops or seminars. For example, when you consider your past you may feel that the things that happened to you would be of interest to people living in the same area today, to those who have a shared history or to people who have experienced something similar.

Organisations that are often looking for speakers or workshop organisers for their programmes include the Women's Institute, the University of the Third Age (U3A), local history societies, craft guilds, parents groups, alumni organisations, environmental groups, libraries and museums, local churches, societies of groups such as graduates or scientists and annual festivals of various sorts. Many of the annual programmes produced by such groups are published on the Internet or can be sent to you by the relevant organisation. They are always prepared well in advance and so, if you feel your contribution would fit in well, contact the programme secretary and arrange a slot for your session. With most small societies, they will not be able to offer a fee but might take you out for a meal in lieu of payment!

Broadcast

When it comes to broadcasting, the BBC may be out of reach for most of us but there are hundreds of local radio stations and

147

hospital radio groups and they are always on the lookout for contributors with something relevant or interesting to say. This might be in the form of a talk or story read out loud, but is most likely to involve taking part in a relevant on-air conversation with a presenter or debate with others. Even if you don't want to take part yourself, you may find you can write out your material in a form that could be read by someone else.

Activity 7

1. Take a topic from your autobiography that would be suitable for any of the organisations mentioned in this section (or one you have identified yourself).

2. Plan out a 20 - 40 minute talk and note any suitable memorabilia or photographs you could use as illustration.

3. If you enjoy the idea (or would prefer to run a workshop or take part in a discussion on the same topic) contact the organisation and set up a contribution for real.

Book publishing

Although there are now options for creating electronic books, for most people writing an autobiography the ultimate aim will be to produce something that is robust enough to withstand handling and being passed down to future generations that you will arrange to have printed and then distribute amongst a limited number of relatives and friends.

If you are more ambitious and feel that your life story could be of interest to a much wider public, you may prefer to concentrate on getting it published by one of the many publishers currently bringing out autobiographical works.

Self-publishing

At its most basic, you could print out your autobiography on A4 paper in a domestic printer, staple the pages together and give copies out.

For most of us, it is worth spending a little money going to a printer or self-publishing Internet company and having 10 – 20 copies of the manuscript bound. You may also want front and back covers created using one of the company's sets of templates or your own illustrations.

Normally it is fairly straightforward once your manuscript is on your computer to upload and then edit the files using the company's software and to receive your basic number of copies a few weeks later.

Some of the decisions you will need to make include:
- Size of page
- Number of pages (very important when trying to keep costs down)
- Type of binding e.g. spiral or plain binding
- Cover – paperback or hardback
- Type of paper
- Font (print character) style
- Colour or black & white if photographs are included
- How many copies to order
- Whether you want the option for further copies (print-on-demand)

- Whether to include an ISBN book number (needed for any future sales)

You can produce eBooks for free on sites such as Amazon but if you want hard copies there are hundreds of companies offering this service and I cannot recommend any personally. The prices cannot be confirmed as they depend on your book details and the level of service you select, but one website to consult is selfpublishingadvice.org which offers a list in their view of the best and worst companies around in 2018. The list is published by ALLi - the Alliance of Independent Authors.

You need to carry out research and read all the small print **very** carefully before deciding on the eventual company you use. In particular, make sure you own the rights and that the ISBN number is in your name. Also – ask for a sample of the paper as this is where online companies can skimp and the results may be very disappointing.

Take care if the company offers you "extra" services at a high price such as editing or marketing your book. Very often, they do not follow through on these aspects or do not do them to a satisfactory standard and you will be left regretting your outlay.

If you prefer a more personal service and simple binding, you should be able to find local printers from your yellow pages or business directories and can call in and discuss your project in person.

*

Activity 8

Using one of the above companies - or another you find on the Internet - work through their help screens by putting in your various preferences to find out what a run of 10 or 100 books might cost you.

Mainstream publishers

The trouble with self-publishing is that there is no real support behind you. If you want to see your book in bookshops and need it well presented, edited and marketed to retailers, the ideal is to have it published by a well-known company such as HarperCollins, Penguin, Macmillan, Bantam etc. or at least one of the many independent publishers.

Publishers come in all shapes and sizes, from very small family firms to giant companies, but whatever their size, the only reason they will be interested in your autobiography is if they are certain it will sell. That is because there are huge costs involved in editing, designing, printing, marketing and distributing a book – especially by an unknown author.

If you are confident that you have an unusual theme or your story will be of interest to a wider audience, you could certainly approach a publisher if they are in this field.

Activity 9

Use the library, the Internet or bookshops to make a list of 10 publishers who publish autobiographical works.

The Submission document

The way most publishers like to work is to receive a brief letter (or email if accepted) explaining why you are contacting them and enclosing a carefully written document known as the *submission document*. This will set out all the necessary details of your proposed book. If they are interested in the idea, they will take the submission document to their next publishing meeting where they will decide whether or not to go ahead.

Most companies publish submission guidelines on their websites or will send you a copy in the post. They usually all ask for similar things and so here is what you are likely to have to prepare for them:

- A provisional title
- A brief synopsis of the book, summarising its content, scope, general approach and any special features
- Your intended audience
- The likely market for your book
- Data on the competition including titles of similar books and how your book fills a gap or offers a different slant
- A full outline of all the chapters
- An idea of its length and, if not finished, when it will be completed
- One or two chapters, to show you can write
- Why you are a suitable author (e.g. you have published before, your unique background etc)
- Contact details and possibly a full C.V. if relevant

Activity 10

1. If you want to have a go (and the worst that can happen is they will say no!), identify a suitable publisher and download or ask for the submission guidelines.

2. Prepare your document and send it together with a covering letter/email to a named commissioning editor (phone the company to ask for this if it is not available online).

Literary Agent

Many publishers refuse to accept speculative approaches from authors, particularly for fiction but often for many other types of book as well. If autobiography falls into this category as far as they are concerned, you may need to use another approach. This will involve being taken on by a literary agent.

Experienced and professional agents act as a go-between between authors and publishers and they will have built up good contacts with various editors. If they believe in your work, they may be able to get it considered for publication. Although you have to pay them a fee such as a percentage of your sales, it may be the only way to get your book published.

Various publications including *The Writers' and Artists' Yearbook* or *The Writer's Handbook* (available in reference libraries) publish lists of agents and the different categories in which they specialise so you should be able to find a few to approach who take on autobiographical books. Send them something along the

153

lines of a submission document, suitably altered to be relevant to an agent.

* * * * * * * * * * *

Conclusion

Although this is the end of the book, it will not be the end of your task as it is now up to you to finish what you started. If you get stuck at any point, go back to the relevant chapter and see if you can find the help you need.

Even if it feels very hard, there is no reason why you cannot produce a body of work that will give you and your family great satisfaction.

I wish you all the very best – and don't forget to carry out the final activity.

And now try this..........

Use this opportunity to identify a problem that is preventing you moving on smoothly with the work in hand. It could be an organisational issue or something that stops you completing a chapter, magazine article, talk or piece of research.

Write it in the form of a statement in as much detail as possible and then create a SMART goal you could set yourself that would go some way towards solving the problem.

If the technique works – repeat it every time you get stuck.

* * * * * * * * * * * *